FEED MY LAMBS

Teaching as Shepherding

Ervin F. Henkelmann

Publishing House
St. Louis

Copyright © 1993 Concordia Publishing House
3558 S. Jefferson Avenue, St. Louis, MO 63118-3968
Manufactured in the United States of America

1   2   3   4   5   6   7   8   9   10   02   01   00   99   98   97   96   95   94   93

CONTENTS

ACKNOWLEDGMENTS

Making a spiritual difference in the lives of children and families is what *Feed My Lambs* is all about. The "hug" of the Gospel has been important all my life, and I'm grateful to a church that has provided so many people and ways to keep God's love and forgiveness in Christ before me and in me. All of us in the church are forever shepherding others. It's great.

In writing this book I've had lots of help and I do wish to say special thanks to the following:

To Art Linnemann, my first principal, a friend and mentor who has shepherded well the vision of the Gospel-hubbed Christian school.

To Priscilla Henkelmann, my wife and best friend and a great shepherd teacher of little ones, who encouraged me lots, critiqued my writing, and made many other things work so that writing time could happen. And to our daughters, Kim, Kari, and Coleen, who each in various ways keeps encouraging me to write and give my writing extra life and meaning.

To the teachers and pastors I've been blessed to work with the past 30 years. It's been a real joy to witness lots of great shepherding and care in action. They're the real fabric of this book.

To Richard Kapfer, who on one occasion was a co-presenter to 1000 pastors and teachers in Texas and made Ps. 78:70–72 come alive for me, and through it and his presentation provided me the basic outline for a 12-chapter book on shepherding.

To the Lutheran Education Association, and its several-year editorial committee, Wayne Lucht, Les Bayer, and Keith Loomans, that nailed me down to do a monograph called "The Shepherding Role of the Christian Day School Teacher in the Classroom." It sets the stage for this book.

To Janet Buckner, a friend and parent of St. John's, Orange, California, who so expertly and kindly stowed each chapter into her home word processor, and smiled and said it was good.

ACKNOWLEDGMENTS

To Ruth Geisler, who patiently and expertly shep-edited and managed to get me back to the last third of the book after my lengthy illness, and who corralled Norris Patschke, Andy Bacon, Dennis Verseman, Gerhardt Meyer, Mary Huebner, Keith Loomans, Larry Sohn, Marvin Bergman, Vic Constien, Rudy Block, Hal Whelply, Duane Hingst, Carl Christian, Dean Dammann, and Gary Bertels to read and review chapters on behalf of their college or seminary classes or district teachers. Their observations were astute. My thanks to each.

Erv Henkelmann

Setting the Shepherding Stage

God's Love: The Great Hug that Holds Shepherding

It's within God's love
    That we find clarity and
        Purpose and
        Peace.
Out of the immeasurable,
    Imponderable ocean
    That is His heart for us,
    And for every person on earth,
We discover what it means
    To be wanted and claimed,
    To be forgiven,
    To be called to a life built
        On faith
        And hope
        And love,
To be His teachers.

God's love is vast, yet near. It's deep, yet a child's sand scoop has it in hand. It's multi-mountain high, but the sands at its base are immediate in their attraction and touch and warmth. It's a worldwide bank open 24 hours and every day and entirely available, one that fully assuages every need, covers any debt, finances any good desire or action.

Realizing that God really cares about me and cares for me is the good news I need to hear every day. He knows me. I'm His. Out of a marvelous love I was born and baptized.

6

As the word of God's love breaks into my day, it brings with it the assurance that all is well. I may have something really bad barge into my next hour, but He is with me and His presence will enable me to cope and to carry, to come out on top, to smile, to have the laugh that is last and lasts.

Word of God's great love is a hug. At times it's a quick on-the-run grasp. At other times it pauses and holds on, it becomes a meaningful squeeze. Still on other occasions, it's a long and enduring clutch with time on hold. The hug steadies and secures. It communicates. It works. The message gets through, and through it we can stand. We need not totter. We can walk for God is at our side. We can run for the Almighty jogs with us. We can stumble or tire, and the Lord is our rest and renewal and will refresh us. It's a great hug to have word of the Father's love made real for us each day.

And nothing makes that love more real, nor communicates it more quickly than word of His Son. Jesus of Nazareth, the one we call Christ and Lord, became the Father's biggest hug. Our heavenly Father gave Him to the world as a real person at a real time in history. Word of the greatest gift He could give, "given for us", is a reach with great love in mind. The warmth and joy of Christmas couples with the victory and life of Easter to hold us, tell us, assure us. Christmas and Easter are arms of truth that embrace us in our greatest need, our sinfulness.

We are sinful and inconsiderate brats. We feature that we have no need for this loving God and His Son. The enormous history of evil and wrong wells up a mass of rejection to the hug. Our inherited and inherent audacity and stupidity turn us away. It's our good fortune indeed that we can't deter God's reach any more than we can cause it. The hug simply is, it always is, and it's ours in spite of our sinfulness, our brathood.

Christ's crucifixion cross has arms. Though in Jesus' time a symbol of agony and death, the cross is now held high with joy and certainty. The arms of that cross reach around the world.

It's this cross-centered message regarding God's love that has attracted ministers into the full-time fray of Christ's service. Those of us with built-in gifts for teaching have been especially drawn to the work of bringing Christ to others. He, too, was a teacher. His

7

parables continue to teach. His lessons on giving and forgiving and praying are taught over and over. His disciples really did the job. They passed the word on, and it is with us today, a tribute to that teaching and to a life and death that backed it up.

As we carry on the task of spreading the good word of God's love in Christ, we look to His Word to direct us. Doing so particularly well and with precision and power is the word *shepherd*. It's the most frequently used image in the Bible for those who have been called to lead God's people. Anyone to whom God has given the responsibility for the spiritual care of His people can be said to shepherd them. God has established the role of the shepherd in the pastoral office in the congregation. Yet in all healthy congregations the shepherding tasks fall on many shoulders. Day school teachers, in particular fulfill Jesus' comand to "Feed My lambs."

We teachers are called to reflect God's loving shepherding. He is the ultimate in shepherding even as He is the ultimate in loving and giving. We wish to mirror Him in all we do and say. We pray that our children and families will see Him in our witness and hear Him as we speak.

Surveying, mining, and claiming the shepherding role of the classroom teacher will serve you well. Your call to teach is indeed a call to copy the Lord, the Good Shepherd. You'll enjoy thinking of yourself as a shepherd in a long line of shepherds, a line that has its origin in Him, a long arc-tracing line that circles back to Him.

Jacob of Old Saw God as Shepherd

When Joseph took Manasseh and Ephraim, his two sons, to see their grandfather Jacob, he heard his sage parent use the precious image of shepherd for his God.

In Genesis 48:15–16 Jacob pronounces a blessing over his son with these words: "May the God before whom my fathers Abraham and Isaac walked, the God who has been my shepherd all my life to this day, the Angel who has delivered me from all harm—may He bless these boys." Jacob knew well the God in whose name he spoke. His shepherding spirit had enabled Grandpa Abraham and Dad Isaac to walk in the way of faith. Jacob knew that the very maker of heaven and earth had shepherded him all his life. Jacob appreciated how God had acted through His messenger and served as

8

the redeemer who pulled him out of the disastrous consequences of his own wrongdoing. Jacob displayed a keen understanding of God when he spoke of Him as shepherd.

Later, when Jacob pronounced his blessings upon his sons, he spoke the 49:24–25 blessing over Joseph: "But his bow remained steady, his strong arms stayed limber, because of the hand of the Mighty One of Jacob, because of the Shepherd, the Rock of Israel, because of your father's God, who helps you, because of the Almighty, who blesses you." In this, the second of the only two references to God as shepherd in the book of Genesis, Jacob again uses this intimate metaphor for the God who had loved him and led him well.

Jacob knew shepherding. It was his vocation from youth. It was the job he performed for 20 years for Laban, his uncle and an experienced shepherd. His shepherding continued when he returned to Canaan where his sons carried on in the same work. Jacob could easily imagine the parallels between God's care and leading and that of a good shepherd, between God's feeding and protection and that given by a good shepherd. He knew the hug. He had felt the Lord's full and warm acceptance. Shepherding was Jahwehlike.

David Tied the Lord and Shepherding Together Forever

David, too, knew shepherding. In his direct reference to God in Psalm 23, he used the shepherd-and-sheep imagery to convey powerfully the loving care of God for His people. He paints a time-immemorial picture for all who would come to know and love the Lord.

The Lord is my shepherd, I shall not be in want.
He makes me lie down in green pastures,
He leads me beside quiet waters,
   He restores my soul.
He guides me in paths of righteousness
   for His name's sake.
Even though I walk
   through the valley of the shadow of death,
I will fear no evil,

9

for You are with me;
Your rod and Your staff,
    they comfort me (Ps. 23:1–4).

David's sheep-talk makes sense. The word *shepherd* was commonly used to describe kings in the ancient Near East, and Israel was no exception. A good leader would seek the contentment and secure the rest depicted in "lie down." He'd find the green pasture that would make life flourish, and his shepherd-rule would revive and protect the subject-sheep. David knew the hug of God. His psalm may well have accompanied a festival of praise at verse 6's "house of the Lord."

The people of Israel knew shepherding. In verses 1 and 2 of Psalm 80 they shout to their Shepherd-God to awaken and lead them with the glory and might He had shown in the exit of Egypt and the promised-land entrance. "Lord," they might have said, "You hugged us once. Hug us again."

Through sheep communique, God knew His people would begin to understand His great love and care. Ezekiel voiced the Lord in chapter 34:11–12 saying, "I Myself will search for My sheep and look after them. As a shepherd looks after his scattered flock when he is with them, so will I look after My sheep." The message of the hug of the Lord was longstanding. He wanted Israel to find swift and decisive action in the embrace of His arms.

Jesus Said His Dramatic Yes to Sheep Talk Too

Jesus knew that His followers would easily pick up on this heritage-deep shepherd-talk. He said His *yes* to it all. He wanted it to be fully clear that He and the Shepherd-God were one and the same. Twice in John 10, Jesus states, "I am the good shepherd." He was indeed the true Shepherd, the Messiah, of whom Ezekiel had spoken, and His I-lay-down-My life-for-the-sheep word was to give extra meaning to the greatness of His hug.

To follow Jesus is to be a shepherd as He was. The eleven disciples on the great-commission mountain got the word to "go and make disciples," and were directed as individuals and as a group to be "baptizing them" and "teaching them to obey everything" He had commanded them. In post-Pentecost haste they jumped into shepherding, and the church was on its way. Each new follower had a shepherd. Each new follower was Spirit-equipped to shepherd others. Acts 9 tells us that "In Damascus there was a disciple named Ananias." He was commissioned to shepherd Saul of Tarsus, to baptize him, to feed him, and to send him into ministry and mission.

Paul and Peter Continued Shepherd Talk

Saul became Paul, and Paul knew shepherding. His Spirit-led pastoral activity brought the Gospel alive in the Mediterranean world of his day and has continued ever since via the New Testament to make the Gospel alive for all of us. Paul knew powerfully the hug of the Lord and dedicated his life to carrying it everywhere.

Paul called the elders at Ephesus to the work of shepherding. "Keep watch over yourselves and all the flock of which the Holy Spirit has made you overseers. Be shepherds of the church of God which He bought with His own blood" (Acts 20:28). These overseer elders were told to shepherd those in their congregational care. A chain was in place and all of us in professional church work or lay leadership are clearly linked into the same shepherding work.

Peter is every bit as renowned as Paul as a giant in early shepherding. Peter fulfills Christ's commission to feed His sheep as he writes his first epistle to the churches scattered across much of Asia Minor. In 1 Peter 5:1–4 he identifies himself with the elders of these fledgling congregations, and then uses the mighty shepherding metaphor to hearten them in light of the great responsibilities and difficult situation they face. "Be shepherds of God's flock that is under your care, serving as overseers—not because you must, but because you are willing, as God wants you to be; not greedy for money, but eager to serve; not lording it over those entrusted to you, but being examples to the flock. And when the Chief Shepherd appears, you will receive the crown of glory that will never fade away."

All who are called to serve as professional church workers can identify as overseers with flocks in their care. Teachers are assigned classes. Teachers in Christian schools are spiritual overseers of their classes. They have flocks. They are shepherds.

Tied as shepherding is to the essence of who God is and what He wants done, it becomes a great gift for the person of God called

11

to do His work to know and to consider sheep and shepherds and shepherding. A teacher of the Lord is bound to be blessed as she counts herself a shepherd. A teacher of the Lord is going to grow as he organizes his ministry around a shepherd-plus-flock model. A kindergarten teacher shepherds the faith development of her kindergartners and does what she can to witness and nurture that faith in the family of each child in her class. A team of parish ministers is certain to be unified if each looks at the other as one who shepherds the spiritual lives of all placed into their care.

God's Gift: The Shepherding that Holds the Great Hug

Shepherding sounds easy enough. It would seem that anyone might be assigned the taking care of mere sheep. No big deal. Couldn't one grasp the basics by getting a few directions from someone who has tended sheep before? Couldn't one . . .

Ah, but . . . and the thinking begins. What does it really mean to take care of a little flock? How easy is it to keep sheep alive and healthy and happy? It's a help to remember some of one's ventures and misadventures in the business of raising something.

Tomatoes, for example. They're pretty simple to grow. Should they be trimmed? When? Where? What's the best way to stake them? Do you feed them, or do you just water them occasionally?

Carrots. Plums. Peanuts. Gardeners, orchard owners, and farmers, each will have a great deal to say about the care and skill, knowledge and dedication involved in bringing in a good crop.

Then there are animals. My favorite classroom pets are guinea pigs. What a wonderful occasion it was when Susie had three babies during the very science lesson I was teaching about mammals and their reproduction. But even though guinea-pig care is very easy compared to tropical fish care, or caring for that spoiled, ill-tempered spider monkey that came to visit my classroom for a semester, there still is a lot to learn about the feeding and cleaning and general care guinea pigs need. Animals of any kind are plenty challenging to raise.

Then there are people. Raising one of them is also seen by some as a pretty easy task. Yet we hear about base neglect, parental ignorance, child abuse. What indignation and anger stirred in my heart

12

when I read of a baby who died in his mother's sun-baked, fully-enclosed car while she indulged in an afternoon of sex and crack in a motel room nearby. What joy, though, in watching a young mom and dad as they lovingly and capably care for their little one. It certainly becomes a full-time task, calling for knowledge, skill, sensitivity, and devotion. It's our hope that through whole and happy toddler-to-teen family education, a mature young adult will emerge, one who also might wisely and selflessly raise and parent a child. That calls for a long and complicated process. People are complex. Tending just one is a big job.

Shepherding people is no small task either. Nurturing the faith of just one little child is a major assignment. Born a sinner as he is, that youngster will fight the process. Being raised in a community and world that daily evidences sin and evil harms and hinders that process. The devil and his evil cohorts will seek to destroy the process entirely. Neglect will occur. Incompetence will take its toll. Tending the spiritual growth and development of people is complex, and it's a process of paramount importance. It has eternal ramifications.

Pastors Can Tell You

Professional shepherds can tell you in a hurry how difficult it is to tend God's people. They cite obstacles. Scores of changes can be identified that make the vocation of parish pastor a demanding and difficult role. Best-selling author/consultant Lyle E. Schaller has written *It's a Different World,* (1987) to provide an overview on just that—pastoring today is a tough job. The mobility of people is a huge challenge to the church. The decline in the stability of the family is a huge problem. *"The percentage of adults who are currently divorced has quadrupled since 1950. The number of couples living together, but not married, increased at least tenfold between 1970 and 1985. The number of children living with only one parent doubled between 1970 and 1985 while the number of two-parent households (with at least one child under age 18) actually declined by over a half million"* (p. 28).

A host of church family concerns present added challenges. Denominational loyalties are fading, and when a denomination is in numerical decline the problem is exacerbated. Shrinking numbers of people lead to shrinking resources and often bring on severe divisiveness and politicized decisionmaking. Expectations regarding church attendance decrease as the competition for people's Sunday mornings increases. Church shoppers judge a pastor's competence, personality, and performance. Church members are apt to be suspicious and openly critical of the shepherd they view as employee rather than leader. Preaching and teaching the Gospel effectively remains the toughest job in the world.

Taking Shepherding Apart

It was a real blessing for me recently to share keynote responsibilities regarding shepherding with a pastor for a convention of 1,000 pastors and educators. Rev. Richard Kapfer presented the Bible's word on shepherding, while I presented the case for effective team ministry on behalf of the shepherding parish and its school. Pastor Kapfer led a two-part presentation on Psalm 78:72.

Shepherding needs heart and it needs hands. It needs the right attitude and the acquired skill. On this base, Kapfer clustered a series of key shepherding concepts for each of the two dimensions. He did a great job, and the extra-nice part for me and this book is that he gave me permission to utilize his outline. His insight was a great gift to me as author. It's also a great gift to all who will enjoy this book and pattern their shepherding ministries on the premises it establishes. *Good job, Dick. Our special thanks.*

Shepherd King David Had Heart and Hands

"He [God] chose David His servant and took him from the sheep pens; from tending the sheep He brought him to be the shepherd of His people Jacob, of Israel His inheritance. And David shepherded them with *integrity of heart*; with *skilled hands* he led them" (Ps. 78:70–72).

From shepherd boy on David handled himself with dignified demeanor. He took great honor in stride and was consistently loyal to his king. With this honor he combined a rare quality of diplomacy. He was clever, astute, and a shrewd politician.

David undertook nothing without checking it out with the Lord. Priests and prophets crop up everywhere in his story. He was a

14

noted poet and great musician for the Lord. He wrote. He prayed. He sang. David not only planned and made preparation for the construction of the temple (1 Chron. 22–23) but also organized the staff of temple personnel, including the musical guilds.

David, of course, did mess up very badly when he "messed" with Bathsheba. He not only appropriated the wife of soldier Uriah, but had Uriah murdered to do so. He also, however, heard the stern word of prophet Nathan and repented. David submitted to the judgment of the Lord. Bathsheba's child died. Sometime later she had another. His name was Jedidiah, better known as Solomon.

Shepherd King David accepted a huge responsibility on behalf of the Lord. God selected Judah (instead of Ephraim) to be the leading tribe of Israel. Through regent David the Lord established His people securely as His kingdom in the promised land. God chose David as His servant and marked him as a member of His royal administration. David was no small piece in God's messianic puzzle. He was a model and example for any who would work for the Lord.

King David performed his shepherd-king work with integrity of heart. His affections were of God. His whole personality was tied to being the Lord's person. He had heart for what God wanted to get done. David did have integrity. He had a great attitude.

Shepherd King David worked with skilled hands. He worked smart. He organized. The military machine he developed was awesome. He was a great warrior and an excellent general who organized and deployed his forces with ingenuity and great skill. David also had keen perception. He looked down the road. He was well-equipped for the job.

Our shepherding tasks as teachers need David's kind of commitment and care. We need heart. We need God's great hug to be an integrally incorporated part of our attitude towards the ministry and mission set before us. Our work on behalf of children and families and their spiritual lives also needs David's kind of preparedness and planning, organization and attention. God's gift of shepherding through us can make the great hug of the Gospel a very real part of people's lives. That takes the best skills we can muster. We need hands.

Read on.

Notes

Lyle E. Schaller, *It's a Different World: The Challenge for Today's Pastor* (Nashville: Abingdon Press, 1987) contains insights into the "new realities" of church life today for church-work professionals.

The Shepherd's Heart

CHAPTER 1

Commitment

Believing, Bound, Blessing, and Blessed

A shepherd makes a commitment. The sheep need care. The responsibilities have been made plain. What the sheep will eat and drink and where they'll do that eating and drinking are clear. The shepherd grasps his tasks as tightly as his staff, and his heart assures all concerned that all will be well with the sheep.

Jesus certainly imagined that the shepherds of His day were committed to their sheep. John records what Jesus said in the 10th chapter of his Gospel (v. 11), "I am the good shepherd. The good shepherd lays down His life for the sheep." Obviously commitment is no small matter. Shepherding is a serious obligation. Life and death are involved. The Christian teacher-shepherd wants to see the youngsters in her care in heaven one day. Spiritual life and spiritual death are involved. She pledges to do all she can to serve as a tool of the Spirit so her students rightly relate to their heavenly Father and believe in Jesus as the very shepherd who gave His life on the cross for them and their salvation.

The teacher's first commitment is to the Lord Jesus. That's where Christian ministry begins. Oswald C. J. Hoffmann spoke about commitment and Christ in an interview printed in the *Lutheran Witness* following his 33 years as the world-recognized speaker of radio's Lutheran Hour, part of 52 years of full-time church work. Upon his retirement in December 1988 at age 75, Dr. Hoffmann was interviewed and the first question asked of him was, "What has kept you going?"

Dr. Hoffmann responded, "I think it's a commitment that you make when you enter the ministry that this is what you're going to do, and it looks to me as if commitment is a necessary ingredient of the ministry. It helps carry you over the rough spots and it also keeps you humble on the days you're riding high.

Commitment to whom? To Jesus Christ. We are not here to promote ourselves. But we identify ourselves with Jesus Christ. That means that our actions have to be in conformity with the Gospel that we're proclaiming."

So the church's teachers believe. They have been called as teaching ministers of the Gospel, and they believe that the Gospel is indeed the best message there is to touch the hearts of people. They believe that faith comes by hearing, and hearing by the Word of God. They believe the Scriptures are the source available for information about God. It's their belief that pastors and teachers carry out the highest function of ministry because theirs is a ministry of that Word of God.

Pastors and teachers make similar commitments. They have similar ministries. Teachers recognize quickly that pastors must be teachers too. Pastors teach a lot. Teachers also readily sense that Christian teaching embraces a good deal of shepherding. They do the very best for those assigned to their spiritual care as they minister with all the plus of personal association that a shepherd has for his sheep.

Teachers Are Committed People

Teachers have a heart for people. They have subjects to teach, lessons to plan, classrooms to keep orderly and neat, but their first business is people. Teaching is a relational affair. First, the teacher gets to know those he is to teach, and their needs, interests, and goals. That's being bound to people and it calls for teachers to be people-persons.

Communication is the lifeblood of teaching. Teachers see people as gifts that God has given. It is through the human ties that grow through relational communication that gift-giving happens. Teachers are daily and deeply immersed in this giving and receiving process, gifts themselves from God to His people. They are people specialists and are clearly committed to students as people.

Impersonalization is unacceptable. Neglecting students' needs for happiness and fulfillment is inexcusable. Building students' self-respect is an integral and pervasive part of the work. Whether a little

20

child in preschool, a kindergartner, fifth grader, middle schooler, or high schooler, each individual is to be seen as a priceless gift. Each is granted a place in our lives filled with high honor and respect. Each is blessed and loved.

Committed to Kids

What a strong picture the John 10 Jesus-words provide for the shepherding teacher. "He calls His own sheep by name and leads them out" (v. 3). It's so easy to see the teacher at work.

"We're going to go out to play now. Randy's row, walk over to the door and line up please." And they do. "When He has brought out all His own, He goes on ahead of them and His sheep follow Him because they know His voice" (v. 4). How similar to the third-graders as they follow Miss Bergt over to church for the weekly chapel service. Shepherds know sheep. Teachers are committed to children. Teachers know kids.

And there's much to know. The shepherding teacher has an interest in children that borders on fascination. Children are wonderfully complex, yet often easily understood and predictable. They are vastly different one from another, yet so similar as they move through a stage or act their age. Children can be a joy and a pain, a blessing and a bane, a breeze and a bust, a delight and a frustration (and all in the same math period).

Every teacher carries about a basket of child development understandings. Into it she places a large and varied collection of things she has learned about children. Her *experience* with children, for example, will provide rich basket blessing. What a valuable thing it is if the "new" teacher has already taught several years of Sunday school, been involved with vacation Bible school for the umpteenth time, served as a counselor for summer day camp, worked in a day-care center, been a baby-sitter since age 12.

Or consider what it means for the basket to have much *common sense,* that special and native judgment that arrives so quietly, but so surely, through one's parental, educational, and community upbringing.

No minor child development-basket blessing is the teacher's *biblical perspective,* that certainty of what God has shared about people through His Word. How truly vital it is to know what it means to be both saint and sinner. What inestimable value it is to realize that children have been created to serve and are equipped by the Holy Spirit to make ministry happen. How tremendous for a teacher to view a child as one that is claimed and called to community as part of the body of Christ, His church.

But into this rich basket-mix goes still more. Carl Rogers belongs there. Although clearly a humanist, his person-centered approach opened new doors for all educators, greatly helping us to understand openness and honesty and the value of self-esteem. Haim Ginott has a place. He taught us how to listen to children and to talk to them with his language of respect. Thomas Gordon is there for helping us to learn valuable skills, to gain understandings about feelings, and to make us more effective in our communications. Don Dinkmeyer and Rudolph Dreikurs are there because of their encouragement process, and for clarifying discipline concepts such as natural and logical consequences. Dr. Spock and Dr. Mom and Dr. Seuss deserve to be there to remind us of how much there has been and how much more there is, for us to learn when the pediatrician, child psychologist, and those who simply know and love children share their wares.

Child-development theories line and shape our basket. Sigmund Freud pioneered well on behalf of child development, biological instincts, and parental influence. B. F. Skinner's behavioral research and the four stages of cognitive-development theorized by Swiss psychologist Jean Piaget add to our knowledge. We recognize Lawrence Kohlberg and the moral-development theory he described, and James Fowler who set up a model for faith development. Each has contributed valuable ideas about children. Each raises important questions. Delving into the theses of these and other theorists in the light of God's Word certainly assists the committed Christian educator in getting to know children.

Committed to Blessing Children with the Gospel

Poured most generously into the Christian educator's child-development basket is the Gospel. Flowing into every part of that basket and soaked into every fiber of the basket itself is the Good News of Jesus and all that it means to those who have heard it, believed it, and come to live in it. The great hug of God's love in Christ brings

22

with it the love and acceptance, forgiveness and communication, empathy and self-discipline that all the specialists and theories have sought. It's there for the having. It's there for the blessing. It's there for the children of the shepherd teacher.

Think about Zacchaeus (Luke 19:1–9). Consider what kind of childhood he may have had and how it shaped him into the adult who climbed that sycamore-fig tree. Being little probably hadn't helped. Perhaps he learned to win by manipulating and cheating. Money spoke loudly, and he knew where he could make a lot of it. What did it matter that he had to consort with the Romans and compromise his heritage and his very being? He had a house and good clothes and good food and wealth. But think about the real Zacchaeus who wanted love and acceptance, forgiveness and communication and fellowship, to be of service to others, to be happy.

Jesus found Zacchaeus. The Gospel finds people. Jesus invited Himself into this chief tax collector's home and life. The Gospel invites the unlikely and unlovable every bit as much as it does those already receiving its strength and power. Jesus not only brought Zacchaeus forgiveness and new worth, he returned his heritage and turned him into a worthwhile person. Lost Zacchaeus was found. The Gospel reaches out to everyone.

Being committed both to the Gospel and children opens up wonderful doors of blessing. Christian family counselors Gary Smalley and John Trent have built on this combination well and have communicated both wisdom and biblical insight to help Christian parents bless kids. Their dedication to the needs children have to be accepted and experience intimacy and affection led them to write *The Blessing* (1986). Their work is certainly a blessing to Christian teachers.

Based on what they have drawn from patriarchal Old Testament stories about being blessed with acceptance and affirmation, Smalley and Trent have identified five key elements as basic components for communicating love to children. The book looks at each in detail. Their operating definition of the family blessing contains all five and reads:

"A family blessing begins with *meaningful touching.* It continues with a *spoken message of high value,* a message that pictures a *special future* for the individual being blessed, one that is based on an *active commitment* to see the blessing come to pass."

Shepherding children begins with commitment to acceptance. The Christian teacher's dedication to children then calls her to demonstrate acceptance. Meaningful touch is important. With a clear eye to the policy constraints and wise cautions that are in place, a teacher finds appropriate ways to hug and touch kids.

Saying special things to kids is important. Good words carry positive power, even as ones that "chew out" and "cut down" carry negative power. Letting Rebecca know that you consider her a swan will empower her. A ballerina she'll be. Calling her a duck won't do it.

Saying to Tom, "You'll make a great lawyer some day," may be the very thing Tom needs to hear so that he will be a great lawyer some day. Getting Tom through law school will take a lot of parental commitment. Getting him through seventh grade English may be the key current commitment!

Blessing a kid makes me remember Messiah, Chicago and a child named John. We called him Johnny. My long summer-Sunday debate with his dad regarding the relative merits of Christian day schools and public schools led his parents to enroll him and his brother at Messiah that fall. He became a spunky member of the fourth grade half of my Grade 4 and 5 classroom. Some 15 years later Johnny shared that he still had a little note that I had written to him. It had suggested he become a pastor some day. Although I had long forgotten the note, it was part of the blessing that a teacher and a school gave to a wiry little kid. John had by this time graduated from seminary, was serving on the seminary staff, and was about to leave shortly for a long tour of duty as a missionary pastor in South Korea. Just prior to leaving, John blessed my hospital bedside following a serious car accident. He brought me an Advent devotion, the cheer of the Christmas Gospel, his smile of acceptance, and his prayer.

Shepherding teachers committed to kids and to their spiritual lives are bound to beget some of those children as shepherding church workers. What a blessing! The rest of the children will include those who become congregational leaders; the many who will be Christian parents, workers, managers; and professional people who shepherd scouts and basketball teams, the Board of Elders, their pastors, their friends.

Committed to Congregations

So very often it is a Christian congregation, or an association of congregations, that makes possible the school in which the shepherd teacher works. A committed company of fellowshipping believers requests a teacher to join them in ministry. They extend a call to be a part of their professional staff. Because they are doing God's work in God's name, and have prayerfully established the position, it is indeed God's call. It's rightly termed a *divine call* or *solemn commission.* God's people issued it.

The Christian teacher's call is to that congregation and, with acceptance of the call, comes commitment to the mission and ministry the congregation supports. What most congregations do can quite generally be summed in listing the following five, classic categories: We worship. We witness and evangelize. We nurture. We serve and care. We fellowship. Although variously described, that's what churches gather to do.

While the teacher may be specifically assigned to the preschool or the sixth grade, and therefore called to nurture, she is also called to all that the parish does as it strives to be the Lord's body and to serve His purpose in a particular place. The shepherd teacher worships and communes and assists in making worship as meaningful and joyous as it can be. Being a part of a choir, or giving a children's message, or serving as a greeter are examples of typical worship involvement.

Outreach is integral. The shepherd teacher is a missionary. The teacher's heart goes out to the Zacchaeuses of the community. Some will be right there in his classroom and tied to a family that needs his evangelism call and prayer. Some will see and hear his missionary witness via community activities such as Little League, the library board, the Rotary Club. Some will come to school for Grandparents' Day or come for the Baptism the teacher encouraged for one of his fifth graders.

Service and care go on regularly. At times it's gathering food or sheltering the homeless. At times it is a Saturday work party to paint the youth house or to plant flower beds. At times it's volunteering as a dishwasher for the Women's Ministries Bethlehem Brunch or making six October stewardship calls on member homes.

Church fellowship is also going on all the time. The shepherd teacher enjoys it, nurtures it, makes it more meaningful in whatever way she can. There's a coffee spot to frequent on Sunday, even if she doesn't like coffee. There's a retreat to attend or a play to direct. There's a retirement party for Hilda at the Miller's house and a volleyball game versus St. Victor's on Sunday evening. Clearly, the teacher can't do it all, but the heart is there to be a part rather than apart, more present than absent.

And there's more to nurture than just our school or preschool or day-care activity. The shepherding teacher sees great opportunity for nurture and keeps contact. He drops by Sunday school classes several times a year. He attends a weekly men's Bible class and occasionally teaches a midweek Bible class. He helps direct the vacation Bible school program in July.

The congregation is a dynamic and busy community. The Spirit is in rich evidence as the congregation worships and serves, teaches and reaches. The teacher loves these people, forgives their failings, is sad when they're sad and glad when they're glad. And each week she writes out a generous check to give back to the Lord—a special thanks for being able to participate in keeping the Gospel alive and growing.

The shepherd teacher has a shepherd's heart and sets aside his life for the sheep. Imagine, however, that you could have someone teaching who is just a hired teacher and is not the shepherd who sees the sheep as his own. So when he sees hard work, or that a brave witness is needed, or that the pay is too little, he abandons the place and its sheep and finds greener pastures and leaves his classroom vacant and vulnerable. He takes off because he cares nothing for the sheep (John 10:11–13).

Commitment is a vital part of the shepherd's work. The flock is in this place, this ministry, this class. It is not over the next knoll. It is here where the Owner has placed him. The flock is not unworthy of the shepherd. If anything, in light of who the true Owner really is, the shepherd is unworthy of the flock, except that the Owner has placed him *here* in this place. Commitment to the flock, then, flows out of commitment to the One who has called the shepherd to His sheep. That Owner, of course, is God. He has purchased all the sheep "with the precious blood of Christ, a lamb without blemish or defect" (1 Peter 1:19). To this Christ and His Gospel and His people the shepherd teacher is bound, bound to be a blessing and bound to be blessed.

Notes

1. "A Conversation with Ozzie," appeared in the January 1989 issue of the *Lutheran Witness,* pp. 6–7. The article contained an edited version of an interview of Dr. Oswald C. J. Hoffmann by Rev. Stephen B. Wenk.
2. Carl R. Rogers, *A Way of Being* (Boston: Houghton Mifflin Company,1980) is a cohesive presentation of a person-centered approach to life. Rogers was a central figure in the field of humanistic psychology for more than three decades.
3. Haim G. Ginott, *Between Parent & Child* (New York: Avon Books,1965) was a landmark bestseller that offered a direct and easily understood method of communicating with children.
4. Thomas Gordon, *T.E.T. Teacher Effectiveness Training* (New York: Peter H. Wyden, 1974) supplied new building-block skills for effective teacher-student relationships.
5. Don Dinkmeyer and Rudolph Dreikurs, *Encouraging Children to Learn: The Encouragement* (Englewood Cliffs, NJ: Prentice Hall, 1963) served as a stepping stone toward the integration of psychological and educational practices.
6. Benjamin Spock, *Baby and Child Care* (New York: NALDUTTON, 1985) was the 40th revision of Dr. Spock's famous book that was parenting's primary resource from the forties on into the seventies.
7. Marianne Neifert, *Dr. Mom: A Guide to Baby and Child Care* (New York: G. P. Putnam's Sons, 1986) is a contemporary source book on infant and child care.
8. Dr. Seuss, *Six by Seuss* (New York: Random House, 1991) includes *And to Think that I Saw It on Mulberry Street* (1937), *Horton Hatches the Egg* (1940) and four other classics by Theodor S. Geisel. It illustrates deliciously the 45 books he wrote and illustrated for children.
9. Sigmund Freud, *An Outline of Psychoanalysis* (New York: Norton, 1949).
10. B. F. Skinner, *Science and Human Behavior* (New York: Macmillan, 1953).
11. Mary M. Wilcox, *Developmental Journey: A Guide to the Development of Logical and Moral Reasoning and Social Perspective* (Nashville: Abingdon, 1979) provides concise summaries of the basic theories of developmental psychology. Includes J. Piaget, L. Kohlberg, and J. Fowler.
12. James W. Fowler, *Stages of Faith* (New York: Harper and Row, 1981).
13. Gary Smalley and John Trent, *The Blessing* (Nashville: Thomas Nelson, 1986) provide both skilled wisdom and biblical perspective to help Christian parents (and teachers) bless children.
14. James Michael Lee, editor, *The Spirituality of the Religious Educator* (Birmingham, AL: Religious Education Press, 1985) shows how religious education activity deepens the lives of religious educators and how they can enhance their own spiritual growth.
15. "How's Your Spirituality?" by Arthur L. Linnemann was published in the March/

FEED MY LAMBS

April 1992 issue of *Lutheran Education* (River Forest: Concordia University) p. 224. Linnemann provides insight into Christ-centered spirituality and its importance for church workers.

CHAPTER 2
Willingness

Bent, Broadened, and Becoming

I love clay. Put a ball of soft, gray clay in my hands, and I'm soon busy and happy. It's a joy to roll and squeeze and shape. Some of my most memorable art periods with children were those in which each child was given the opportunity to play with a big handful of clay. Most kids also like clay and enjoy molding it into something recognizable and special. I'd often begin teaching about clay by asking the children to make a mushroom. Their hands would soon squeeze part of the ball into a stem and allow the other portion to "mushroom" above forefinger and thumb to become a top to flatten and round and smooth.

Clay reminds me of people.

It's clay's malleability that connects me with people, and it's especially easy for me to see little kids as globs of clay. Observe them with a preschool teacher they love and trust, and you can enjoy the pliancy and readiness for change of which I write.

But then there's little Roberto. He clearly has his own view on what he's going to do or not do. Roberto can be pretty unmovable at times. His preschool teacher says he's a strong-willed child. He's that all right, but he's only been in this world for three-and-a-half years, and it's a pretty bewildering place. He'll loosen up. You can already see how his teacher's warmth and encouragement are beginning to break through.

There's a little Roberto in each of us, in each teacher and in each candidate for shepherd work. We draw back. We refuse. We resist. We also, however, recognize and respond to the great capacity for acceptance and change that people have within them. That's what we will consider in the second great description of the shepherd's heart as we think about people and clay and willingness. We re-

29

member Jeremiah going down to the potter's house to watch the potter working at his wheel, to catch the picture there of Israel as willing clay in Potter God's hands. The Lord shaped the destiny of the people of Judah. The Lord has shaped His people in all times and places. He shapes His shepherds.

The commitment to be in the Lord's work and to be serving His people contributes greatly to the willingness that is part of the shepherd's heart. The desire to be a shepherd includes a willingness to bend the way shepherds bend.

It's always fun to think of Jesus' disciples as shepherd clay, and to consider them on a malleability scale. It's not hard to see educated and considerate Luke as a willing worker. He displayed great heart in the loyalty and friendship he gave to Paul. Paul in turn would have given Mark much lower grades. He was deeply disappointed when Mark deserted him and Barnabas on their first missionary journey. Paul flatly refused Barnabas' proposal to take Mark along on the second journey. Mark may have been more like his close associate, Peter.

Peter had plenty of Roberto in him. He had some classic moments of unwillingness in the followership department. We church workers have to love Peter. It's so easy to see ourselves in his unwillingness to let Jesus wash his feet, his unwillingness to admit to the high priest's servant girls that he was Jesus' disciple, his post-Pentecost unwillingness to realize that God wanted the Gentiles, too, to be His people.

But Peter bent. It took Jesus' strong words, several rooster crows, and a dramatic rooftop vision in Joppa to loosen him up, but Peter bent and broadened and became what the Lord wanted in a follower and a leader. God *gave* him that willingness. It's good for us to view our willingness as a "given," a gift that becomes ours as the Holy Spirit works the clay, patiently kneading us with His unbending Law and with the sweet and powerful Gospel and His Sacraments.

Peter identified willingness as a key element in the business of shepherding. His appeal to the elders of his congregations was clear: "Be shepherds of God's flock" and be "serving as overseers—not because you must but because you are *willing,* as God wants you to be; not greedy for money, but eager to serve; not lording it over those entrusted to you, but being examples to the flock" (1 Peter 5:2–3).

Do you hear the Gospel in Peter's words? You aren't a willing shepherd because "you must," but because you *are*. Peter is telling us that willingness comes with the territory. Furthermore, he imagines it to be an eagerness to serve and a desire to be an example. It flows as a "given," as part of the grace that is ours in the Gospel.

I love to go back to Dietrich Bonhoeffer's *Life Together* and read and reread the many things he has to say about living in the flock. The "community" he calls it. "Therefore, let him who until now has had the privilege of living a common Christian life with other Christians praise God's grace from the bottom of his heart. Let him thank God on his knees and declare: It is grace, nothing but grace, that we are allowed to live in community with Christian brethren."

If that can be said (and it surely can and must) about living together as Christians, how much more can it be said about leading Christians and working together as a team of Christian leaders? A Christian teacher is steeped in grace all the time. God has clearly blessed her. God has clearly given her a "territory." That grace-full "territory" is a flock of children alive in their baptismal, Christ-claiming grace. That "territory" includes the coshepherds and lay membership, ministers all, who are there because of Jesus Christ. They come to each other only through this same Jesus Christ. They are tied together in a unity of grace because that's what the Father had in mind when He sent us His Son. That's what the Son had in mind when He sent us the Holy Spirit.

Christians are free to be. We're no longer looking for our salvation. We have it. We don't have to search out ways to love others and how to live with them in concord and peace. We have the Way, Christ Jesus. Through Him we meet God Himself. Through Him we meet our brothers and sisters and love them and forgive them and serve them and get to understand them. It comes with the territory. When we "got" God, we got a lot of givens. As we receive His mercy we learn to be merciful. As we receive His forgiveness we are made ready to be forgiving. As we receive His help we're bound to become more helpful. All that is part of the Good News. We are incredibly free. We are free to be.

When Nate joined our day school faculty at St. John's, we assured

31

him that he was not only becoming a part of a congregation of God's people, but that God had all kinds of good things waiting for him. God was already there ahead of him and had been since 1882. In Christ he could very confidently realize that all the love, forgiveness, help, and appreciation he'd ever need was already there in full measure, knee-deep.

And it was important that Nate was bent. Already from his born-in-parsonage days he was bent. His Baptism started things off. His family kept things going with its accepting warmth and loving direction. He was bent by congregation and college, peer and spouse. Nate has, then, overwhelming reason to believe in the people of his new congregation, and in their ministry and mission, *and to become* one of their willing shepherds.

Nate could, of course, be concerned about finances. After all, he and Jennifer have a two-year-old and a second child due shortly. He'll need to plan with care, and to accept early on, that a parish teacher will not have many of the niceties of modern-day Malibu.

At the very same time I can share with Nate that in my 30 years of parish and interparish ministry, there's always been income enough to manage the year in and manage the year out. Investments, extra houses, expensive cars, and extensive vacations have not been possible, but neither have they been necessary in order to do ministry and be happy. They more likely would have been deterrents.

Church work needs full-time workers, and shepherding church workers work more than full-time. So it simply has to be if extra visits are made, if extra notes are to be written, extra prayers prayed, extra plans laid. Congregations find the way to balance things for their shepherds. It's the church's job to see that a teacher will not have to worry about finances, will not have to incur debts, will not need to take on part-time employment. Teachers' attention is far better given to the people-tasks that are a part of each day.

Swinging the financial pendulum to the other extreme is to imagine the church worker who gets absorbed in seeking or enjoying wealth. That's not good either. Peter wanted shepherds who were "not greedy for money." Shepherds are free to be. Peter covers both contingencies nicely as he continues, "Humble yourselves, therefore, under God's mighty hand, that He may lift you up in due time. Cast all your anxiety on Him because He cares for you" (1 Peter 5:6–7).

The shepherd's heart trusts that the God who balances the universe (so perfectly and well, thank you) will manage quite nicely to bring about an appropriate balance in his shepherd's checkbook and life, and the life of his family. The shepherd's real willingness is to let the Lord and His people handle the anxieties that come along.

It finally becomes apparent that the shepherd's willingness to shepherd is closely tied to her spirituality. Paul made it clear to the Ephesians that it was "the gift of God's grace given" (3:7) that made it possible for him to "preach to the Gentiles the unsearchable riches of Christ," (3:8) "and to make plain" (3:9) the way God works among His people. A willing heart flows out of a willing spirit. That willing heart is not ours because it comes naturally. It's a given—a given from God. In chapter 4 of Ephesians (vv. 1–16) Paul goes on to show how God made provision for those in the church to work together in unity and to grow together into maturity.

Marva J. Dawn, a marvelous theologian, author, and speaker, wrote a fine series of *Lutheran Education* articles regarding the spirituality of Christian teachers. In the periodical's second article (November/December 1988) she states that, "Our spirituality is based on the reality of the grace of God which can be objectively known by means of the gift of the Holy Spirit's renewing of our minds. As we respond to the truth of God's love for us, we are also enabled to respond with love to God and others whether or not we feel like it." What is of God *comes* to us from God.

Dawn, however, also concludes "that certain spiritual practices enable us to perceive grace more fully, that specific training fosters the development of Christ-like virtues in our character, and that particular habits make it more likely that we will experience God's presence rather than simply know it in our heads." What we do with worship and discussion and study and song and joy makes a difference. How willing our hands are to serve relates to what's going on in our spiritual hearts. How malleable we are to the Potter's touch on Sunday makes a difference to the kind of ministry vessel we are on Monday.

So "because of His great love for us, God, who is rich in mercy, has made us alive with Christ," (Eph. 2:4–5a) and because Christian teachers daily wade knee-deep into the reality of parish-life grace, there's an incredible variety of ways for God to work His willingness in their lives. The following examples open us to realize what all the Gospel-bent shepherd is given to broaden and strengthen that spirituality base. Each reader, bent in the Spirit, will imagine additional examples as well.

• There's church worship on Sunday and God's presence in liturgy and lesson, sacrament and song, in the messages for adults and children, in the gathering of His people.

• There's evening preparation for tomorrow morning's fourth-grade Christian learning lessons with Scriptures in hand, guides to guide, prayers to aid, the Gospel to pull out, the Gospel to set up (and to enjoy in advance).

• There's that warm weekly group that meets on Tuesday evenings for an hour to dig deeply into the Word with that grand old Spirit-led layman from St.Matthew's.

• There's the morning faculty devotions that will be led next week by Miss Sallach. They'll be Gospel-good—and fun too.

• There's Pete and Sandra's wedding next Saturday. Pastor Fred's message, and the whole service, will be a blessing to our marriage too.

• There's the children's message on Luke 5:1–11 that's in the works for the Sunday after next. It'll be great to be able to do that again. Always makes one really study a portion of the Bible.

• And there's three weeks from Sunday when I get to teach the adult information class for Pastor Constien. There's a lot of getting ready with all those Bible references to review and present, but what a blessing it'll be to be involved with the Word.

• There's the parish staff overnight retreat next month at Forest Home. Becky's songs will be special, as will Dick's devotions, and Loren's doing three sessions on Colossians.

• There's the Rich Buhler book *Love: No Strings Attached* that I'm reading. Rich is right on, and it's fun to pore over his practical, colorful solutions on how to love ourselves and others.

• There's my un-daily daily Bible reading. (Missed four out of seven days last week, but I'm all the way to Romans 8.)

• There's *Renewing the Family Spirit,* the Dave Ludwig video course from Concordia Publishing House that the faculty is studying. It really is helping me develop stronger ties with my daughters.

• There's evening's closing eyes, tired body, and repentant heart wrapping up the day's ups and downs, praying over joys and remorses and think-singing, "Hold Thou Thy cross before my closing eyes, Shine through the gloom, and point me to the skies . . . "

Each of us is God's clay. He keeps us in His hand. The Christian teacher is greatly blessed by God's grace to be working and living in His hand, to be daily squished and massaged by His Spirit and power.

Each of us is our own clay too. We're in charge of our social and emotional lives, our intellectual and physical selves. We are each in charge of our own charge. So much of what has to do with our health and happiness has to do with how willing we are to care for ourselves.

The effective shepherd teacher needs a heart for good physical health. There's weight to lose, teeth to floss, lungs to protect from tobacco smoke, vitamins to take, and sleep to sleep. We need exercise, fresh air, good foods—and moderation in regard to junk foods, sweets, and alcohol. Each day we do little favors for our bodies, and we may take some very dramatic steps like surgery and hospitalization, so that we can go about our work and play unencumbered.

In the same way, we need willing hearts regarding emotional health. There's stress to understand and eliminate. There's value in getting to know oneself and better understand one's personality. There's honesty to face, and truth to grasp, regarding our relationships. There may be need for a workshop on change of life, counseling about sexual dysfunction, a book about marriage, psychoanalysis, or hospitalization for depression. There are people we need to forgive. There are people we need to forget. There is much we are free to do that can help us mold our personal clay.

The shepherding teacher strives to be professionally alive and well. Doing graduate work, attending conventions and workshops, participating in professional associations, and reading professional books and periodicals are things we are either doing or not. Teachers are either growing or going stale. Shepherding of children and families is too important to put into the hands of teachers who are not on the grow. So is the shepherd's heart bent as it looks to be broadened and busy in becoming the best it can be.

Notes

1. Dietrich Bonhoeffer, *Life Together* (New York: Harper & Row [now Harper-Collins], 1954).
2. "Spirituality and the Christian Classroom" by Marva J. Dawn is found in *Lutheran Education* (Nov/Dec 1988), River Forest: Concordia University.
3. Rich Buhler, *Love: No Strings Attached* (Nashville: Thomas Nelson, 1987).
4. David J. Ludwig *Renewing the Family Spirit* (St. Louis: Concordia Publishing House, 1989) is the basis for a video course also titled *Renewing the Family Spirit* (St. Louis: Concordia Publishing House, 1991) that presents an innovative yet practical guide to understanding and resolving differences in the everyday life of the Christian family.

CHAPTER 3
Compassion

Brats, Bandits, and Bandages

"Jesus went through all the towns and villages, teaching in their synagogues, preaching the good news of the kingdom and healing every disease and sickness. When He saw the crowds, He had *compassion* on them, because they were harassed and helpless, like sheep without a shepherd" (Matt. 9:35–36).

The needs of children vary. Child to child, school day to school day, school to school, community to community, the needs differ greatly. Nevertheless, for most teaching shepherds the workday needs of the classroom flock will be quite routine. Compassion will not be on constant call. It certainly may have to be there on a moment's notice, but compassion punches a selective time card. That's fortunate. It's not easy to deal with a lot of emotion on any kind of regular basis. Most teachers don't.

But that's not to say the shepherd need not be compassionate. Working with people, any people, does call for compassion. When the needs become special, the sensitive shepherd has special feelings to match. The harassed and helpless, those desperate or terribly depressed, those in crisis and crying, summon emotions to suit. Shepherd Jesus was quick to respond.

Blind-beggar Bartimaeus received mercy and sight. Moved and troubled by Mary's weeping at the loss of Lazarus, Jesus wept. A short while later He exulted in Lazarus' being brought back to life. Christ healed the 10 who had leprosy. He put His arms around little kids and took them on His lap. Although cross-wracked with pain, He lovingly found Son-care for His mother, and later, at death's door, took time to hear and bless the criminal's cry. Christ lovingly exemplified compassion. He taught about it too.

Through a parable about loving one's neighbor, Jesus brought together a man half-dead, crumpled and bloody, with that unlikely-candidate Samaritan the whole world now identifies with compassion. The Samaritan's feelings drew him to care and to help where others had not. He did what he could, disinfecting and bandaging. Jesus' story-hero cared enough to carry his neighbor to haven and rest. Compassion pulled out those coins. Compassion promised payment for the care yet to come. Compassion created a bond beyond and provided the big help needed.

This same parable spoke to teachers on a retreat in Indiana one August. A young pastor named Lowell Thomas was speaking. His sermon spoke of "Brats, Bandits, and Bandages." His "brats" drew on the broken bonds between Jew and Samaritan. There'd be brats in the school year ahead. They would include kids, of course, but there'd also be parents and colleagues and pastors. Sin bandits would swoop down and hurt and steal. They'd harm and damage relationships. Bonds would weaken and occasionally break.

But teachers had bandages. They could bind up problems and help things heal. It would take effort. There'd be cost involved, but the One who told the parable would be with them. Jesus had not counted the cost, even a cross. For each one present, Christ was the Good Samaritan who brought the care and healing of the cross. Their ministry was to do, then, as He did, to be good Samaritans for others. The Gospel power of that memorable message still warms my heart and stirs it to go the extra mile to care for those with special needs.

Shepherding teachers are bound to encounter some pretty scruffy and unlovely lambs. They'll need something deep and strong to move them, to give them big hearts that will reach out and help in spite of whatever scruffiness exists or unsavory condition is found, to be compassionate Samaritans.

I often think about Wayne.

Lamb Wayne

Lamb Wayne was pretty helpless. He was a beaten puppy. Sad, sunken eyes reflected depression and defeat. A too-long belt hitched up his too-large, K-Mart slacks. Wayne was skinny and dirty and backward and tired. He seemed lifeless. He was limp. He was also a little curious.

Who is this tall person with the tie talking to his mom? Why had he been so persistent? He knew Mom didn't want to have him come in. Somehow he had managed to get Mom out of her bed, and he is talking to her as if he likes her. How could he? Mom looked awful again. And she smelled. Couldn't he smell the wine? Why didn't he notice things? He didn't seem to see her hair and her brown fingers and her brown and broken teeth.

"Wayne, c'mon over. I've got something for you too," the man said.

And Wayne came closer, cautiously. Someone special sat at the table where he had wolfed his cereal. The bowl and spoon still sat on the table.

"Wayne, let me show you this list. These are the things I'd like you to bring to school next week. I'm going to be your teacher." The man gently created space at the table.

Wayne came a little nearer, but he was still uncertain. Would his new school over by the church off Addison be better? How he hated school.

"Wayne, are you a lefty?" How did he know? "I wondered that when I saw your spoon," the man continued. How does he know my thoughts? And why is he here? No one's come here before. He does seem kinda' okay. He makes me smile. I wonder what it will be like to have a man for a teacher?

That home visit to Wayne's house made a huge difference in the relationship I had with Wayne. And Wayne did have a good year. The same Lord-led compassion that caused me to make an uncalled-for house call was the same compassion that spurred me on to work hard with Wayne, to find some worth in him, and build on it so that he and his mother would each see their worth and go to work with me.

Teachers all have their Waynes, and when we look at children as spiritual beings, all children *are* Waynes. Every child exhibits the scruffiness and unlovability that comes with sin. The shepherd teacher views each with the compassion that reaches out as Christ does.

Jesus' approach to individuals was never built around scolding or condemning them as sinners. That was true even of gross sinners like Zacchaeus and the Samaritan woman at the well. Instead of viewing them as "brats," he simply saw them as sheep who had no shepherd.

The passion with which the shepherding teacher will pursue opportunities to speak and witness the Gospel to children and parents is certainly related to the compassion she has for their souls. Allowing lost sheep to stay lost will not be the modus operandi.

Jesus' parable of the man who owned a hundred sheep (Matt. 18:10–14) is addressed particularly to the spiritual loss of children. He taught it to His disciples as a follow-up on the very dramatic better-to-have-a-largemillstone words that clearly established His high value of children and their faith. With the discovery that one sheep was lost, the parable's owner would certainly halt everything, set aside His work with the 99 other sheep, and concentrate on the hunt for the one that had now become 100 times more valuable. What made that sheep extra valuable was that it was lost.

Wanting Brigette Baptized

Marcia Phillips had 24 second graders. During the month of September she established that all were baptized except for Brigette. As she told her story later, Mrs. Phillips said, "Maybe what really helped is that I had just one child that year who wasn't baptized."

It became a topmost objective for Marcia's first quarter parent-teacher conference. She *had to* talk to Brigette's parents about Baptism. Brigette's mother, Sarah, shared that she had been baptized as a baby, but that she had not belonged to a church since she was about 10, a time when her parents had moved. Austin, Brigette's dad, quietly stated that he didn't think they would pursue the matter. He had never belonged to a church and was not baptized. He was not currently imagining any tie with the school's congregation.

While Marcia was a bit disheartened by the conversation, she knew she had sown a valuable seed. She kept Brigette in her prayers. Two special things took place to water and warm that seed for sprouting.

The first was a delightful happenstance. It occurred on a Sunday early in December when her second-grade class served as the choir for the 8:00 a.m. service. Most of the class came to sing. Brigette did, too, and Sarah and Austin were present as well. The beauty was that two young children of a new member family were baptized in that service, and Mrs. Phillips had the opportunity to say a quick: "I hope you're still thinking about Baptism for Brigette." She smiled and received smiles from Sarah and Austin in return.

Then came the accident. It took place at Austin's store when he slipped at the top of a high ladder and took a bad fall. Several fractured ribs and a broken hip and a hospital stay resulted. Marcia and her husband Ken visited Austin, and during one visit Marcia asked if she could say a prayer. She held his hand and asked for the Lord's blessing on Austin, his healing, his business, his family, his daughter. Austin was moved.

Marcia told Pastor Wendt about the accident and asked him to stop by the hospital. His visit and prayer, too, were received well. Marcia also made a large get-well card and each of Brigette's classmates added a note and their names. Quite a number of children mentioned the Lord and spoke a prayer in what they wrote. Brigette reported that her dad really liked it and said that what she wrote was very special to him too.

Pastor Wendt stopped in to see Austin several times during his convalescence at home. It was already clear that Austin had turned a special spiritual corner. He began attending church during his crutches-and-cane days and decided to attend the pastor's information class. Brigette was baptized around Easter on the same Sunday that her dad was baptized and confirmed as a member of the congregation. Mrs. Phillips served as Brigette's sponsor.

The shepherd teacher cares deeply about children and families. She has a great respect for each person as an individual God has created for good purpose. When a child in her care is not faith-related to the Lord, compassion moves her to take spiritual action. Her compassion is not merely sympathy or pity. She's a missionary on a spiritual mission. Her compassion calls her to prayer and to imagine herself as part of prayer's answer.

The shepherd teacher's compassionate care calls her to be generous. She goes out of the way to hug the unhuggable. She scrounges up time and energy to do things that clearly communicate she has God's heart for people. She has a generous schedule. A telephone call at home does not find her harried and hurried, even though she is indeed harried and hurried.

The shepherd teacher's compassionate heart is forgiving. His lifestyle is forgiveness. He is constantly encouraging his school children to be quick to be sorry and to be quick to forgive the sins of sister and brother. He is generous in the amount of time it takes to clearly communicate the Gospel, God's no-strings-attached love, at times when a child has erred in some way. He is a person, himself, who says "I'm sorry." His class hears his repentance and knows that it speaks absolution. Each of his students knows that he is quick to apologize. His too-angry response to a student's misbehavior is followed shortly by a repentant request for forgiveness. His compassion reflects that of his Lord and longs for the great hug of acceptance that little ones, too, communicate on behalf of their loving Father.

It's true. When you work with people, you are bound to run into some that are brats. And it's true that the people you work with are bound to run into bandits. But won't it also be true that whether he is dealing with hard-to-love kids and parents, or ministering to people when they are sick, distraught, or dying, that the shepherd teacher's compassion will be there to reach for bandages? When children and families seem harassed or helpless, like sheep without a shepherd, he can't pass by. He's moved to help. There will be bandages. Compassion says so.

CHAPTER 4

Gentleness

Bundled, Befriended, and Brightened

Shepherds are gentle. They may be swarthy, hardy, and unsophisticated, but we still see them as gentle. Shepherds may have rough hands, crude manners, and little education, but they remain typed in our minds as tenderhearted, kind, and caring. Their reputation is impeccable. Shepherds care about the sheep and lambs in their care.

Shepherds aren't cowboys. They're not on horses shouting, shooing, roping, and branding. They're not forcing and flogging. Shepherds are in the midst of their flocks, in touch and close. Their rods and staffs and slings are only to protect. Sheep are not for beating and prodding. They're to bundle and befriend and to bless. Those who care for them really care.

Isaiah's 40th chapter begins with "Comfort, comfort my people, says your God. Speak tenderly to Jerusalem and proclaim to her that her hard service has been completed, that her sin has been paid for, that she has received from the Lord's hand double for all her sins." Isaiah writes with hope and promise as if the Babylonian exile is nearly over. He comforts the exiles and the spiritual Israel of all times with the promise of deliverance from sin through the incarnation and eventual death of the Messiah. Isaiah is into the Gospel, the "good tidings" (v. 9) about a Sovereign Lord characterized by both strength and gentleness.

This Lord "comes with power, and His arm rules for Him." This is a strong God who has the ability to deliver and to restore. He has the strength to strengthen.

But this Lord is also gentle. "He tends His flock like a shepherd: He gathers the lambs in His arms and carries them close to His heart; He gently leads those that have young" (Is. 40:11). The Lord of Isaiah 40, the one who wants His people to be comforted, reminds them that He is gentle and caring, like the shepherd.

The picture is such a good one for our God. "He tends His flock." He looks after His sheep. He cares. They receive His full attention. "He gathers the lambs in His arms." God's strong arms are ready to bundle and embrace. The arms of the great hug lift up the lambs and hold them fast. Shepherd God then "carries them close to His heart." God draws His own to His heart. The Gospel clarifies that God loves us. His heart is so good. It gave us His Son, a lamb Himself, carried ever so certainly to the cross and to the resurrection by the strong arms of God's love.

The picture is a perfect one for the shepherding teacher's heart. The teacher desires to be as loving as His heavenly Father. He has heard God speak about love and has heard the apostle Paul's famous introduction to words about love: "And now I will show you the most excellent way" (1 Cor. 12:31, the verse before Paul's great description of love).

"Love is patient, love is kind" (1 Cor. 13:4). Sounds like gentleness, doesn't it? "It is not rude, it is not self-seeking, it is not easily angered, it keeps no record of wrongs" (13:5). Love is obviously strong, but its strength is in the full care given the other person's welfare and feelings. It's of God, and love certainly is a close cousin to gentleness. Both are clearly a part of the shepherding teacher's heart.

Some Gentleness Brightens Jennifer

One morning Jennifer's dad had a little problem solved by gentleness. His problem was third-grade Jennifer. She wouldn't get out of the car. School would begin in two minutes. Dad was late for work. Jennifer was distraught. She was crying. She was not going to school. Dad had tried everything he could. He was at his wit's end.

He came to my office for help. Just a year ago he had come with a different problem, a much larger one. Jennifer and her little sister, Erica, were being divorced. Along with their father, they were going through the pain of a mom who was checking out, a mom who had been leaving her family for more than a year and was now cutting away with finality. Jennifer's big need at that time was to see that

44

she was not the cause of that marriage's demise. This morning's difficulty was much, much smaller, but it loomed large to her.

I thought about my options. Stern command might be employed. Physical power began edging up the priority action poll. Punishment might work. There may be some reward that would ransom the situation. But kids with tears, though-be-they tears flowing from ducts of defiance and self-centeredness, need quiet solutions. They need the gentle touch of a Solomon. They need to be understood.

Jennifer was about five minutes late to her first class. She needed to be heard. She needed an ear, one that could hear her feelings. She had to have someone hear that it was no small thing to not have her book-club order with her. Her teacher had been very clear. Beyond today she'd wait no longer. The deadline was now. Jennifer was positive that she would never get that book. Jennifer was at her wit's end.

Jennifer received some gentle ministry that morning. I'm glad I got to be there for her. Jennifer was heard and understood. She was assured. She was gently led to her classroom, just slowly enough for eyes to dry and for confidence to return. Here she was met by more gentleness, her teacher's. There really is grace, even with book orders.

Gentleness is special. What a preferred way to be treated midst the other options. For some children life is tough. Harsh and cold winds blow at kids. Hunger hurts. Lack of self-respect wounds. Courage can dry up. Yes, at times it is just a perception problem, but one that happens to be attended by strong and important feelings.

Gentle voice and gentle look are not to be confused with being wimpy or weak. Gentleness is born of great strength, the strength that believes in God's care and is willing to work and wait for its arrival.

Even in the defense of the faith, Christians are enjoined to be gentle. Recall how the apostle Peter put it: "Always be ready to give an answer to everyone who asks you to give the reason for the hope that you have. But do this with gentleness and respect" (1 Peter 3:15). If this is the way God expects us to treat those who are outside the church, how much more wouldn't He look for us to be gentle and respectful inside the church.

Co-workers need our gentleness as we go about our various responsibilities. A curt reply may seem appropriate, but recognize the way it closes conversation. A sarcastic cheap shot may catch a sideline chuckle, but see how chins drop and eyes turn away. Stern and demanding people can get things done, but that doesn't mean we're going to like it or like them. Briskness, sharpness, and harshness all drive people away.

Our team ministry efforts as church staff need the warmth and caring that comes from the gentleness of the shepherd heart. How congregation staff people minister to one another sets patterns and tones for the whole flock's ministry. How we work with shortcomings and mistakes with one another will likely be the way the membership will work with ours. The gentleness involved in striving for understanding, in looking at both sides of every issue, and in being respectful will bring us peace and unity, harmony and happiness. That's a lot.

The shepherd is gentle. Shepherding is a sensitive business. Those are real live sheep in the flock. They're wonderful creatures. One must marvel at them and appreciate them for all that they are, all that they aren't, and all they can possibly yet be. They'll be brightened as the shepherd handles them and befriends them. There's good cause to be gentle.

CHAPTER 5

The Servant Attitude

Bought, Borne, and Bearing

Shepherds tend sheep. Yes, when all is said and done, there *is* a shepherding bottom line. What the shepherd is all about is summed up easily and well by what the job is all about, taking care of sheep.

Shepherds not only have to be committed and compassionate, caring and gentle, they also have to be ready to do the work. Along with having a heart for the sheep, they must have a heart for the work. They need to enjoy taking care of sheep. Shepherds need servant attitudes. The sheep have their inestimable value, but it's not just the sheep that count. What matters to the owner is that those sheep are getting the care. The owner is paying for shepherding. Shepherding counts.

The prophet Ezekiel was really a heads-up person in a lot of ways. A gifted and capable person, an amazing man of God, Ezekiel could grasp large issues and deal with them by using grand and compelling images. God had a bone to pick with Israel's leadership, and Ezekiel was the man to put it together, the one to make things understood and to declare God's Word with clarity and punch. Catch the picture in the 34th chapter of the book that bears his name.

"Woe to the shepherds of Israel who only take care of themselves! Should not shepherds take care of the flock? You eat the curds, clothe yourselves with the wool and slaughter the choice animals, but you do not take care of the flock" (Ezek. 34:2–3).

Shepherding is not for making a living off the sheep. Whether government or temple, official or priest, Ezekiel wanted institutions and their ministers to know the difference. He spoke directly. You're either in it for people or you're in it for yourselves. Ezekiel elaborated. He went on to identify the shepherding that was not getting done.

"You have not strengthened the weak or healed the sick or bound up the injured. You have not brought back the strays or searched for the lost. You have ruled them harshly and brutally. So they were scattered because there was no shepherd, and when they were scattered they became food for all the wild animals. My sheep wandered over all the mountains and on every high hill. They were scattered over the whole earth, and no one searched or looked for them" (Ezek. 34:4–6).

If the sheep are no longer being served, things really come apart. Those in charge have become careless and uncaring and their work with the sheep shows it. Important things are not happening. The basics aren't getting done. There are weak ones being ignored instead of being strengthened. There are the sick who are staying sick because no one is doing a thing about it. There are those who simply aren't around, and no one seems to care. Still others are in trouble and in big danger and nothing is being done about them either. When those in charge care more for themselves than their charges, sheep will become food for wild animals; they will be "dead meat."

So it is in congregation and classroom if the servants in charge are not serving. The neglect shows. Concerns are unmet. People begin complaining and begin to leave. When shepherding is neglected, families soon drop worship, forget the Lord, find the world, and become "dead meat" for the devil.

Every Church Worker a Minister

Church work is not just for giving and collecting salaries. Nor has the Lord decided to call people together simply to be caring for buildings and programs. A congregation isn't a country club. Its workers aren't just preachers and teachers, or those who set up activities for kids and youth and singles and seniors. The coach is not just a coach. The principal is not just a manager. The science teacher is not just a subject-matter specialist. Each worker is a minister. All are servants.

The classic Bible passage that establishes that every believer is a spiritual worker is 1 Peter 2:4–10: "As you come to Him, the living

Stone—rejected by men but chosen by God and precious to Him—you also, like living stones, are being built into a spiritual house to be a holy priesthood, offering spiritual sacrifices acceptable to God through Jesus Christ." From kid to older adults every Christian is a brick for building. In all that they are, do and say, Christ's followers stack themselves up to God in daily service. He's the Cornerstone. The Holy Spirit designs the plans and directs construction. God's people all are involved in the spiritual work to get God's jobs done. How much more we need to emphasize that every congregational employee has spiritual components that are part of the day's work. How wonderful when the church custodian is at daily devotions with secretary and deaconess, with teacher and pastor. How much cleaner floors and carpets will be when they're viewed as witnesses that God's people are walking on them to their spiritual work.

Paul shows the Ephesians how God made provision for those in the church to live and work together in unity and to grow together into maturity. "It was He (Christ the Lord) who gave some to be apostles, some to be prophets, some to be evangelists, and some to be pastors and teachers, to prepare God's people for works of service, so that the body of Christ may be built up until we all reach unity in the faith and in the knowledge of the Son of God and become mature, attaining to the whole measure of the fullness of Christ" (Eph. 4:11–13).

Church work is a spiritual business. Ministry builds up the body of Christ. Spiritual gifts are to be used for the body, the church, and haven't been given to be exercised individualistically. In the second chapter of Ephesians, Paul says "the whole building" (with Christ Jesus Himself as the chief cornerstone) (Eph. 2:20b), "is joined together and rises to become a holy temple in the Lord. And in Him you too are being built together to become a dwelling in which God lives by His Spirit" (Eph. 2:21–22). The church is clearly for spiritual growth. It prepares its people to prepare its people. The church is people "speaking the truth in love" so that they "will in all things grow up into Him who is the Head, that is, Christ" (Eph. 2:15).

Christ, our true Head and all-powerful Son of God, certainly "did not come to be served, but to serve" (Matt. 20:28). As we grow closer to Jesus, we grow closer to the servant attitude. As we continue to hearken to the "big-hug Gospel" we are headed right into servant

49

work to be people who put God first, others next, and themselves last.

Once Jesus had to pointedly straighten out disciples James and John on this very matter. Their well-meaning mom had come with them to Jesus with a plea. "Mrs. Zebedee & Sons" had power in mind. They figured it would be great to be on top. What they didn't reckon was that Christ was into things quite upside down. His servanthood eyes saw the top as the bottom. "Whoever wants to become great among you must be your servant" (Matt. 20:26).

The teaching shepherd has a genuine heart for servanthood, one that thinks little of the cost involved. It's a heart that imagines a lifelong career of trusting that the servant way is the way to go, of believing that being a full-time church worker actually works, of feeling certain that those famous financial ends will be met, that it truly will be possible to be happy being a servant.

Lambs to Be Served Too

The teaching shepherd acts as a servant to children as well. The Lord's little ones aren't for "lording it over." One time, "An argument started among the disciples as to which of them would be the greatest. Jesus, knowing their thoughts, took a little child and had him stand beside Him. Then He said to them, 'Whoever welcomes this little child in My name welcomes Me; and whoever welcomes Me welcomes the One who sent Me. For He who is least among you all—he is the greatest' " (Luke 9:46–48). The little and insignificant in the eyes of the world are truly great in the eyes of Jesus. A little kid may not count for much to those who run banks and corporations, but to the Lord who knows hair counts and whether a sparrow has fallen, a child counts a great deal.

When the disciples rebuked the people who were bringing babies, Jesus called the children to Him and said, "Let the little children come to Me, and do not hinder them, for the kingdom of God belongs to such as these. I tell you the truth, anyone who will not receive the kingdom of God like a little child will never enter it" (Luke 18:15–17). Jesus clearly was not too busy to be blessing little kids. Jesus considered them totally worthy of His time.

The church, too, looks upon children as important. Its schools and child-care centers say that. Its programs for scouts and children's choirs and teams and summer day camps announce that kids count. Its baptismal font so declares. Children are for serving. They are valuable to the Lord. They're valuable to us.

Caricaturing the Servant-Shepherd Style

The servant-shepherd style can be described in many ways. One method I've used is to have a class imagine that an able cartoonist is asked to come up with a caricature to do the job.

The artist might head straight for the mouth. Why not emphasize the mouth? Sketch a cavernous cavity. We are quick to speak our assessments and even quicker to present our guaranteed solutions. Advice rolls out fast, even when unrequested.

Catch the comedy of it. Hardly has a troubled and weary soul expressed word one, and he's hearing a diagnostic discourse and several concomitant prescriptions. We do love to orate, to share the wonderful wisdom we alone have been privileged to amass. Some of us diesel on and on and deserve especially well the catchword caption of "wind bag" or "big mouth." All of us are too intent on ourselves at times and too unaware of the other's actual need.

Dietrich Bonhoeffer's *Life Together* (p. 97) reminds us that, "The first service that one owes to others in the fellowship consists in listening to them." Just as love to God begins with listening to His Word, so the beginning of love for the brethren is learning to listen to them. People are looking for people with ears. How sad if the caricature for Christians has little ears, ones sedately covered with saintly headsets or stopped with pious plugs. Far better if those ears might be large, God-sized, and good.

The eyes will register the listening that's going on. Draw them with care. They're large, too, for they have much to tell. They say, "You count, my friend, and yes I am hearing what you're trying to explain." They're eyes intent, but unjudging. They sparkle warmth and acceptance. They say, "Yes, I'm ready with my gentle and supportive response. I've heard what was on your heart."

The hands are ready too. They're not limp or lifeless. Nor are they clenched or clawing. The artist captures hands of helpfulness. Bonhoeffer (p. 99) notes, "The second service that one should perform for another in Christian community is that of active helpfulness." So often this first means a little errand, a deed hardly worth mentioning. But with every raised hand will grow the confidence that here is a person who cares. Hands that can stoop to pick up litter or blow little kids' noses get to wipe tears. Hands that touch sagging shoulders and quickly take up their neighbors in a circle of cooperation and prayer get to pick up telephones that God has dialed as He sends people with petitions and claims, with needs noteworthy and weighty. They're His hands, the Carpenter's hands, sure and ready, ready to enfold the lost lamb. They're His hands. You can see the scars.

Bonhoeffer (p. 100) goes on. "We speak, third, of the service that consists in bearing others." His scriptural touchstone is, "Carry each other's burdens, and in this way you will fulfill the law of Christ" (Gal. 6:2). The caricature has shoulders stooped and strong. They're generous shoulders, and across them is a wooden yoke cut and carved by the Carpenter Himself to fit and pad snugly and securely with no rub, no scrape, no irritation. Worthy ropes extend toward things that must be borne, but the artist has left loads undefined. It's not a big box or bag that needs bearing. It's not a beam. It's no cargo. It's a brother.

The burden for the shepherd is a sheep. He may have to pick that sheep up and pack it. It's sick. It's been injured. But really that burden is easy. It's a breeze. The hard burden is the one that deals with this animal's stupidity and stubbornness, its inability to comprehend or communicate.

Shepherding Christians bear one another. What they carry is often no fun. Carrying a brother's narrowness and hardheadedness is a frustrating load. Oddities abound. Thoughtlessness teems. Insensibility and apathy are in strong supply. Inability and incompetency are present too. Weaknesses are plenteous. Friction and frustration ensue. Confusion and conflict and collision occur. All are loads to carry with wisdom and love. They call for a ministry of patience, endurance, and fortitude. All will spawn lament and complaint, drooping shoulders, sinking, repining, depression, and surrender.

And the shepherd servant encounters direct sin as well. The burden of groundless gossip is heavy. The malicious lie saps strength. Dishonesty destroys ties. Deliberate indifference and contemptuous harangue can kill plans and spirit and joy. But these, too, are burdens that can be borne. Forgiveness is not just another load. It's a wonderful load, one to prize as a privilege. Bearing sins is Christian work. Forgiving sins is what Christ's cross was all about. The shepherd servant who has been good at listening, active in helpfulness, loving and faithful in bearing, will be well-equipped to do the greatest ministry too. She will get to bring the Word of God to those who have hurt, to those who have hurt and are sorry, to those who have hurt and are sorry and have turned toward God. The shepherd rejoices. This is special work. It's strengthening the weak. It's healing the sick and binding up the injured. It's finding the lost. It's brightening the day, and for such he was bought.

Principals Are Head Shepherds

Being a principal of a Christian day school is a chief-shepherd kind of job. One certainly gets involved with teacher-shepherd servant variables, with strengths that become so strong they end up as weaknesses, with weaknesses that turn into wonderful assets. To shepherd well a faculty of five to fifteen is to know what all is involved in ministering to people.

Teacher sheep can be lonely and scared. They can become stressed and seriously depressed. Teachers suffer losses of self-esteem just like kids. They can be angry and impatient, and can strike a child. Some live it up. Some give it up. There are those who cry and complain, some who eat too much, those who insist on correcting kids' papers during the faculty meeting, and those who rarely correct kids' papers and fake grades. Some have bad marriages, have spoiled kids, and get traffic tickets. They can be lazy, unappreciative, and have bad breath. They're people. Their administrator(s) minister to them even while they minister to others. They are sheep, too, and they enjoy being led by one who has a servant attitude. Often administrators are wonderful examples for teachers to watch. They've usually become head servants because of servant hearts. The success of their work and their schools is often closely related to the way they minister to people. Learn from them and minister to them too.

The Shepherd Servant and Family Ministry

My first principal was not only an exemplary parish and school minister, he was clearly a family minister as well. His wife, who'd just exchanged classroom for motherhood, was also a family minister. During my year-long internship in their parish school I was often a guest at their table. The meals were great, but I was being served a far-more significant "food." I was privileged to observe and experience a young servanthood family at work. It was good to be in their house, to be warmed by their acceptance. Ministry was not only a constant part of the day's conversation, it was evidenced in the listening and speaking. Helpfulness was going on all the time. Openness was a hallmark. Art respected Vernette and Vernette respected Art. They had a good thing going.

I soon began to see this family as the kind I wanted to one day enjoy. Servanthood was not only preference, it was also a reality. Teachers of Jesus who taught daily of how He emptied Himself when He became a servant could also live as He had lived. They could be loving and submissive as He was and watch it work. They recognized daily that a healthy marriage partnership demands give-and-take. This was not the old joke, the male's one-liner that says, "I give and she takes." This was a very real place for a balanced interdependence to be practiced.

Mutual give-and-take is necessary for happiness. A person must always be willing to give up something of his own desires and needs in order to build a relationship with another person. Community is built inside one's house in the same way it is built outside one's house.

The shepherd teacher realizes that a key way to build the church, that is the congregation, is to be building it family by family. Family ministry gets into the shepherd teacher's blood. It's practiced. It's preached.

Basic to this ministry of family is the shepherd servant's appreciation and understanding of grace. Grace is a relational matter. Our Christian faith is a grace-based relationship with God. His design for family relationships is for them to be lived out in a climate of cross-won grace and forgiveness.

I love the many things Jack and Judy Balswick have clarified in regard to Lord-led family life through their book *The Family: A Christian Perspective on the Contemporary Home* (1989). They present a view of the contemporary family that integrates social-science research, clinical insights, and biblical truth. They conclude that "A family based upon law is a discredit to Christianity. The meaning and joy of being a Christian would be deadened if we conceived of our relationship with God in terms of law and not grace. The same is true in family relationships. As both the individual and family live, law leads to legalism, whereas grace provides a freedom from legalism. In an atmosphere of grace family members act responsibly out of love and consideration for one another" (p. 26).

The Balswicks see a family's covenant of grace ruling out law as the basis for their relationships. They do not, however, rule out rules. Committed family members "living in grace will accept law in the form of patterns, order, and responsibility in relationships" (p. 27). Grace calls for orderliness and regularity to be present as a way of loving others in the family, rather than as means of limiting or repressing them. Just as God has loved us by giving us the Ten Commandments, parents love their children by establishing good and consistent rules.

Grace-ful families experience a mature commitment for one another. They establish an atmosphere of grace that embraces acceptance and forgiveness. Thirdly, the Balswicks view the resources of family members as being used to empower one another. This empowering they nutshell in the following: "TO SERVE AND BE SERVED."

Jack and Judy Balswick call this empowering the "action of God in people's lives" (p. 28). "The Spirit of God indwells believers and enables them to enable others. As this spiritual growth goes on in family members, it is possible for them to serve and give to each other in unlimited ways. Family members will use their areas of strength to build each other up" (p. 29). God's way is for one person in the family to help another person in the family to mature. That's ministry. God's plan is not for us to find ways to control one another. That's the opposite of ministry. That's puppetry.

As the shepherd teacher grows and matures in relational family ministry, his heart calls for him to enable others to enjoy the same. He desires to see family ministry alive and well in all the homes of his students. He teaches servanthood daily. Over and over he connects servanthood with Jesus. It's part of being a believer. It's entwined with being His follower.

The Chief Shepherd Jesus walked servanthood's road. From manger birthplace to borrowed tomb He set aside the amenities. He listened to Mary and made wine. He listened to His disciples before teaching them parables. He heard out Satan and told Him to get lost. Christ helped and healed. He reached out. There were disappointments and tears, anger and frustration. He spoke gentle words and hard words. Christ came to serve, and in Him and through Him we inherit a shepherd servant's heart. He's bought us as He's borne us and borne the burden of our sin. He's empowered us to be the bearing ones, to follow in His way.

Notes

1. Oscar E. Feucht, *Everyone a Minister* (St. Louis: Concordia Publishing House, 1974) is a thorough examination of the biblical priesthood role of the Christian person.
2. Dietrich Bonhoeffer, *Life Together* (New York: Harper & Row [now Harper-Collins], 1954) includes a chapter (4) on ministry which describes seven special ministries vital to Christian community, p. 90.
3. Jack O. Balswick and Judith K. Balswick, *The Family: A Christian Perspective on the Contemporary Home* (Grand Rapids, MI: Baker Book House, 1989) provides an integrated view of the family based on biblical truths, social-science knowledge, and clinical insights.

Toward Part 2

This book is about teaching. It's about what teachers do and how they do it. It's about response. An attitude of commitment, willingness, compassion, gentleness, and servanthood equips the shepherding teacher mightily. Now what will be the response and what will that response be like? Will it work?

Dedication is essential, but what if it is merely an entree for the dull and drab? Learners need M-I-C-E. Not much happens if there is no *M*OTIVATION. Learning begins with the desire to learn. Then, learning is limited without *I*NVOLVEMENT. Active interest, an ownership, helps learning. Furthermore, what teachers hope to accomplish is greatly slowed without *C*ONCENTRATION. Both teachers and learners need to be into *E*VALUATION. Without follow-up teaching and learning suffer.

Given two fourth-grade classrooms in the same school, both with essentially the same textbooks, tools, and techniques, and even the same number of kids, you'll still have dramatic difference. Children can register delight on one side of the hall and dread on the other, even if both teachers involved are dedicated and caring, willing and working.

Zeal is mighty in the business of spiritual shepherding, but it's not enough. Personality counts. One shepherding teacher cajoles and castigates. Another enables and entreats. One prizes the playful. To the other it's a pain. She prohibits the pleasurable and has little time for pleasantries. Each has a style, has brought together a package of personalized practices and procedures. Every good teacher has developed a collection of devices that work. One shepherd has skilled hands. The other has unskilled hands.

Teaching is an art. Top-notch teaching calls for artistry. One of my favorite speakers and writers on the subject is Dr. Louis Rubin, a professor of education from the University of Illinois. In his book *Artistry in Teaching* (Random House, 1985), Rubin provides a well developed and practical strategy for improving the quality of teaching. He points out the need for skills:

> Two facts, in the main, distinguish the strong teachers from the weak: They manage whatever techniques with great skill— that is, they are able to use a device expertly, so that its usefulness is maximized—and they utilize these skills in appropriate contexts. How well a teaching strategy is used, apparently may make more difference than the strategy itself. This "feel" for the right thing at the right time is the benchmark of expertness (p. 5).

Teaching is a profession with purpose involved. We call it education—the process of imparting or obtaining knowledge or skill. The teacher is the educator, a specialist in the theory and practice of education. The professional teacher adds in-service training and experience to gifts and teacher education in order to be good at what he does. Teaching involves workmanship. There's quality in this craft, and a lifetime can be involved in becoming a respected member of the guild.

This book focuses on a distinctive kind of teaching. We call it Christian for it is done by those who believe in Christ. We call them Christian teachers, and we think of them as specialized professionals in the field of Christian education. They're not simply teachers who are Christians. Rather, they are people who have given their lives to be vessels of God's truth to others. They've become immersed in the use of the Bible as the source and norm of their knowledge of God. They seek to be ever-better instruments of God as He has revealed Himself in His Word. Christian teachers are professionally committed to communicating His Spirit to the human spirit, for He must enter the human spirit to give life.

Still further, the focus of this book is on professional teachers of the Gospel. It strives to be a Gospel-driven teachers' handbook so that the words of the Bible will be properly understood and used to convey the truth of God in Jesus Christ.

The professional shepherd teacher prays for the ability to skillfully communicate the Gospel and to care for it as the special spiritual power that it is. I enjoy pointing to a book called *Power Beyond Words* written some years ago (1969) by the noted Christian educator Allan Hart Jahsmann in order to establish this point:

In order to receive the revelation of God in Jesus Christ it is necessary to study and communicate the Sacred Scriptures as Gospel—Gospel in the general sense of doctrine concerning Christ.

In this broad sense the whole Bible is the Word of Christ and the Word of the Holy Spirit, who is the Spirit of Christ and of God the Father. Martin Luther recognized that "all Scripture, when rightly viewed, has to do with Christ." He is "the Truth and the Life" and therefore the Word of divine revelation behind all Holy Scripture, the Alpha and Omega. "If you dwell within the revelation I have brought," said Jesus, " . . . you shall know the truth" (John 8:31–32 NEB).

With God's Word in hand and His Good News of Christ in heart, we will proceed to describe the hands of the shepherd teacher, to consider the array of skills that are involved in being effective Christian teachers. You read it earlier—God's gift of shepherding through us can make the great hug of the Gospel a very real part of people's lives. That takes the best skills we can muster. We need hands.

Notes

1. Louis J. Rubin, *Artistry in Teaching* (New York: Random House, 1985) is written for those who are in education programs and who will be teachers tomorrow. It's for those who believe teaching can be an art and whose goal it is to make themselves artist teachers.

2. Allan Hart Jahsmann, *Power Beyond Words* (St. Louis: Concordia Publishing House, 1969) is a time-honored and stimulating study of the ways by which God speaks and teaches through those who tell and teach and interact. In the foreword to his book Jahsmann wrote, "God is eternal. The truths of His Spirit and Word do not change. But the world, which needs the Word and Spirit of God, is changing rapidly. And the church's ways of communicating with the world can change and may need to. There have been many ways of teaching in the past, and there are many different theories of teaching today. Not all of them contradict one another simply because they are different. At the same time, not all ways of teaching are equally helpful for all times and purposes." True in 1969. True for today and tomorrow.

The
Shepherd's
Hands

CHAPTER 6

Gathering the Flock

Bidden, Banded, and Brought

It's a pretty obvious mark of a shepherd. He gathers his sheep into a flock. In order to move his woolly subjects from the pen to the stream to the pasture, he'll first bring them together. It would be one comic and very weary shepherd who'd endeavor to deliver one sheep at a time from brook to brow, or from knoll to valley. An effective shepherd deals in flocks. The welfare and safety of all is as much the job as the care for one.

Teaching is like that. It's done in groups. Certainly a tutor is great at times. What a blessing for the child who needs remediation. One-on-one instruction to learn how to play the flute or to drive the family car is nice. It's also selective and expensive. The home-schooling parent has many pluses to offer her child, but she also gives up a lot of inter-student motivation and involvement, relational growth, and a wealth of experience and fun. The peculiar genius of teaching is working a group, capitalizing on rich and varied interaction. Teachers are flock people.

The shepherd teacher recognizes that God has gathered her flock. At times the class of children assigned to her teaching care is a strong reflection of the families the Lord has already drawn into the congregation. Often it bears a definite resemblance to the community. Always it represents a distinct little congregation itself, a segment of believers to be nurtured in the faith, a segment of near-believers to be established in the faith, a segment of unbelievers to be won to the faith. In whatever way the school-as-church has drawn these families together, it is ultimately God's gift-answer to its prayers, its witness, its work in His name.

Whether by printed brochure or the yellow pages or parent-to-parent testimonial, the invitation has gone out. The school's name itself can bid families to become involved in spiritual education. Christ Community, Child of Christ, and Risen Christ are clarion calls. Episcopalian, Lutheran, Catholic, and Christian are additional names that announce God's church at work. People know that God's people are behind it. They are its teachers, its day care staff, its core. Through them God gathers.

School ministries invariably illustrate church mission work at work. Parents and students have heard Jesus call, "Come, follow Me and I will make you fishers of men." They have left their net pursuits and followed Him. "Come and see," they have said to their brothers and sisters, friends and passers-by. They have visited the school, observed its teachers, and they have enrolled and stayed.

Each child can tell a "gathering" story related to enrollment. At times the linkage is fairly routine. Perhaps an older brother attended, or his dad attended as a child. At other times parents can tell of the careful community study they made in order to decide on a school that was just the right Lord-based educational spot for their child. It's good for a teacher to know how God gathered the children in her care, how His "voice" was heard. It's important to realize that He has a plan and a purpose for each youngster, to be in this classroom, at this time, and with the particular shepherd or shepherds this school community provides.

It's also important for the children to realize that the Lord has bidden them to be here. They are special and God is calling them to be His. They are here at this special place, banded together with others who are special too. God is bringing them along. He has brought them into His family of believers. He wants them to be His special people, to be His salt, His church.

Brent Came and Stayed

Several years ago I received a letter from Brent. It was just prior to his eighth-grade graduation from our school. He had come to St. John's three years earlier. His parents were divorcing. His father would be moving to the other coast. A private school for their sixth-grade son seemed a good idea. The teachers would be caring and helpful.

Brent's letter is precious. It speaks of spiritual growth. It affirms our work in Christian schools. It helps us see a particular point to which God brought a child that He had bidden to be His.

Dear Mr. Hinkelman and St. John's Pastors,

I am writing to tell you thank you for teaching me during this past year about Christ, and His word, His kingdom, way, life, the priceless gift He has given to us, life, death, friendship, gossip, trust, etc., etc., etc.

Everything which you have taught me, I hope to apply in my daily life as I grow.

I have learned from you, that when I am feeling down, etc. I can pray to Christ for His love and support, I have learned what to do when I have realized I have committed a sin, etc., etc.

"Everything" you have taught me can be applied in my daily life—by what you have taught—I have learned what to do in almost every situation, and when I don't know what to do—I can count on Christ's support and help!

I really am thankful for what you have taught me—and I'm sure I was taught it by you for a reason—I may not know now but I'm sure it's part of Christ's plan for me—so I'm not going to ponder over the question, or the question of what I am going to do in my future—because I know I'll know when it's time.

I am now not afraid of death either, if I come down with a serious illness, cancer, etc.—I now know that it would be for a reason—maybe to teach someone else something, etc. But I would not be afraid, because I now know that when I die— I will be in heaven with Christ—with no more problems, fears, etc.—and for this knowledge I cannot thank you enough!!!

I could write another hundred pages of what I have learned from you—just to write this page it took only a minute because the words just seem to flow (overflow more likely)!

Thank you very much for what you have taught me, and I know I will grow even stronger in my faith by learning and growing more in Christ everyday!

Brent Packard
P.S. Thank you for letting me be confirmed!

Brent came and stayed. Although his parents did not join our church, Brent did. He went on to the high school the congregation sponsors jointly with its sister churches in the county. He faithfully attended worship services. Through his witness, an older brother joined the congregation. Through one another God bids His sheep to come in.

Jerry Came Because Jerry Wouldn't Live Long

It was only my third year in teaching, but I could tell that Jerry's mother had a lot of confidence in what I might do for her fifth-grade son. She wanted him to be treated like any other child. He needed to be seen as special too.

Her eyes said more. She knew something she wasn't telling. Jerry had a disease. He couldn't hold a pencil as well as other kids. He spoke more slowly. He read more deliberately. He couldn't throw and catch like boys his age.

Jerry was a good-looking kid, but his forehead was prominent and rounded. It projected forward, the mark of a hydrocephalic child. He was a bright kid, but his intellect was weakening. Jerry's incurable disease brought him to Trinity. His parents knew he'd not live for more than a couple years. They wanted a warm and caring school where Jerry could be a kid and where Jerry could get ready for heaven.

I loved Jerry deeply. He was special. Recess was close to his heart, and I gently passed him hundreds of junior-sized footballs. He was proud of what he managed to master physically, even though it was far less than other boys. He listened intently as I taught about Jesus. He was fond of his new Bible and was pleased to read it aloud. Being absent a lot and getting behind his classmates was frustrating. Laboring with uncooperative hands was often defeating. Jerry got depressed at times too. I left Trinity at the end of that year. Jerry left it two years later. I left to teach in nearby Chicago. Jerry left to be with Jesus.

Jerry was unique. He became a part of my classroom flock to receive care and patience and understanding. He came so that he might be a regular kid, which he surely wasn't. He came because he was going to die. Through family and church school, teacher

65

and child flock, God gathered him to His body of believers and to Himself.

God invites and gathers. He brings us the lambs and sheep and gathers them to Himself.

John 10 and Jeremiah

God's sheep gathering is described in the tenth chapter of the Gospel of John, the Good Shepherd chapter. "I have other sheep that are not of this sheep pen. I must bring them also. They too will listen to My voice, and there shall be one flock and one shepherd" (v. 16). The church's shepherds gather those whom the Lord has first gathered in order that the Lord might feed the flock on Word and Sacrament.

God is indeed the gatherer of the sheep. He places us over His gathered ones in whatever capacity it is that we shepherd. Through the woes of His prophet Jeremiah upon faithless shepherds, God declares, "I Myself will gather the remnant of My flock out of all the countries where I have driven them and will bring them back to their pasture, where they will be fruitful and increase in number. I will place shepherds over them who will tend them, and they will no longer be afraid or terrified, nor will any be missing" (Jer. 23:3–4).

Just in case anyone might miss the tremendous significance of the gathering which He had just announced, the Lord goes on in verses five and six to declare another of His important Messianic prophecies. "The days are coming . . . when I will raise up to David a righteous Branch, a King who will reign wisely and do what is just and right in the land. In His days Judah will be saved and Israel will live in safety. This is the name by which He will be called: The Lord Our Righteousness."

Gathered to Be Fed

God gathers His flock to provide the food of His promises—the Gospel that invites and strengthens, that bands together the ones who believe and follow.

The sheep come together. Whether to Sunday's sanctuary or to Monday's classroom they come, and they come for a purpose. The sheep come together where they can expect to find food. Shepherd teachers know that their classroom flocks gather daily to be fed.

Teachers Plan, Manage, and Instruct

To feed the student sheep in her class, a teacher dedicates part of each day for worship and prayer, instruction and study.

Like the other time slots of a school day, these spiritual-growth portions involve advance planning, classroom management, and the instructional process itself. The teacher needs to be an expert in all three categories.

Planning. The teacher sorts and plans objectives, needs, and strategies in the initial planning of the school year. The more careful and considered this planning, the more fruitful the year is apt to become. A variety of questions to do with gathering the flock need to be addressed.

• What amount of time will I schedule for opening worship and the Christian learning class? Should I plan another time slot just for Bible reading? How about closing devotions? What can I do to make them special for the kids?

• Should I plan to do a human-care service project with the children? How about one a quarter?

• Could my room students sing as a choir for Sunday worship?

• Wouldn't it be a good idea to take my kids to the sanctuary on occasion? How often and for what purpose?

• Shouldn't we do a field trip this year that is tied to spiritual instruction? Where should we go?

Management. The rules and procedures a teacher plans will make a difference in the gathering for classroom worship and school chapel service. What can the teacher do to help the class bond?

• Could outdoor education become more of a youth ministry retreat?

• What can the teacher do during August home visits to begin spiritual bonding?

• Could students take turns leading prayers each day?

Instruction. As the teacher plans instruction, she might ask:

• How might a new student seating arrangement make my Christian learning class presentations more effective?

- What can I do to help the students who have no Bible background?
- How can I utilize those great Bible story videos the Sunday school purchased?
- What can I do to make the memorization of Bible passages effective and fun for everyone?

Like a wise pastor who retreats annually with the parish leadership to plan a good year for the congregational flock, the wise Christian teacher "retreats" annually to plan a good spiritual-growth year for the classroom flock. She realizes that every part of the day relates to the Christian education she is providing. The time and energy she puts into developing a warm and accepting classroom community is spiritual insurance. It's a key aspect of flock gathering. Much of what genuine Christian education is all about is bound up in the gathering and shaping of the flock.

Earl Gaulke, a long-time editor of Lutheran publications for Christian education, wrote a summary paragraph for an article in the Fall 1990 issue of *Issues in Christian Education* (page 9) that says it well.

> Christian education, therefore, is a matter of living the faith through loving and forgiving in the Christian classroom; including activities not only for learning the data of the faith and reciting it to the teacher, but also for speaking the Word to one another in meaningful life situations. The goal is to build a warm and supportive community in which fellow Christians may be encouraged even to "confess your faults to one another and pray for one another, that you may be healed" (James 5:16).

Dr. Gaulke emphasizes the need for spiritual education to be life-directed as well as being Christ-centered and scriptural. He calls for genuine communication. He wants Bible content to be directed purposefully toward desired outcomes in the lives of the learners.

Community Building Skills Are Crucial

The hands of the teacher shepherd need the skills to build a relationally-strong flock. Pulling children together into a life-changing Christian community is the task. Openness, sharing, and mutual commitment will be its hallmarks. Communication skills, modeled and deliberately taught, are essential. (These will be covered in Chapter 10.)

Respect is the watchword. It's a response to estimated worth. Respectful students have identified a higher value, and something has clicked. They desire to respond in a positive manner, to give honor. We often speak of this as a "treating process." "She treats Mrs. McDonald with respect."

Respect engenders respect. A child tends to be as respectful as those he most respects. Teachers who speak respectfully to their students motivate respectful responses. A respectful and orderly climate may well be the primary ingredient in the development of an effective school.

I've identified five basic expectations that produce increased student maturity and prompt acceptable behavior.

- We respect God.
- We respect our teachers.
- We respect ourselves.
- We respect our classmates.
- We respect our facilities.

As the shepherd teacher illustrates the meaning of these expectations, teaches how this respect can be given, and wisely balances the level of expectation, the flock gathers in a special way. They bow their heads and fold their hands at prayer—because the teacher has demonstrated respectful prayer demeanor. They address the teacher properly and raise their hands politely—because the teacher has explained and practiced respectful procedures. They keep their books and belongings neat and clean. The teacher has taken the time to talk about this and provided incentives. They speak to one another, and about one another, with a measure of respect. That's what the teacher expects. They don't litter or scribble on their desks. The teacher explains the benefits of a neat environment.

With healthy and helpful respect in mind the flock can venture beyond the immediate fold. The heads-up shepherd thinks through the teaching and precautions needed to move the flock. A walk to the city library three blocks away requires planning, management, and instruction. No regimentation or authoritarian action are involved. Just clear expectation. That's good teaching. That's an alert and wise shepherd.

The sheep are invited to do their best, to behave well. They've been bidden to gather for this lesson or that new game. The sheep have banded together well. They care for one another and for the one who cares for them. They care how much the teacher knows because they know how much she cares. They've been brought along. They're further than they were yesterday. They're closer to where the Shepherd and the shepherd want them to be.

Notes

"Effective Christian Educator: Biblical Perspectives," was published in *Issues in Christian Education,* p. 9, Fall 1990. In this article Dr. Earl Gaulke stressed the importance for spiritual education to be life-directed. Bible content needs to be directed purposefully toward the lives of the learners.

CHAPTER 7

Protecting the Flock

Besieged, Bundled, and Bastioned

Kids are besieged. Certainly today's children have tremendous advantage over their historic counterparts, but they're still very much under siege. As the littlest ones of the family, community, and nation, they simply do not command a lot of power. Kids have precious little oomph when it comes to the bigger decisions in life. That matters less when the big people in their lives love and care, understand and guide. It matters a lot, however, when those adults of influence are selfish and insensitive, manipulative and greedy. Or uncaring. Permissive. Overbearing. Ignorant. Children to such are pawns. They become nonpersons. For some adults, children are toys. Because these adults and attitudes exist, problems for kids exist.

Time, the weekly news magazine, cited the siege well in its October 8, 1990 cover story, "Suffer the Little Children." The article had both a world focus and an American focus. While people of the United States cherish the idea that they cherish their children, there is overwhelming evidence that speaks the opposite. America's legacy to its kids includes some bad schools, some terrible health care, deadly addictions, and a great deal of indifference. Just consider the woeful statistics that *Time* compiled to describe a single day's worth of destiny for many American children (p. 42).

Every eight seconds of the school day, a child drops out. Every 26 seconds, a child runs away from home. Every 49 seconds, a child is abused or neglected. Every 67 seconds, a teenager has a baby. Every seven minutes, a child is arrested for a drug offense. Every 36 minutes, a child is killed or injured by a gun. Every day 135,000 children bring their guns to school.

A teacher working with children sees the siege at work. Thinking of each student according to whole-child needs is to realize the many ways in which attacks may come. Some beleaguerment is small potatoes. Kids can handle it. Some of it is protracted and devastating. Some just hurts. Some damages and destroys. Do children need to be protected? Consider the negatives kids face according to the following six areas of child development as you formulate your response.

The Siege Can Be Physical

Think of the physical and realize that children continue to be beaten up and battered. Malnutrition and hunger are very real for many. Nearly one in four American children under age six lives in poverty. Handicaps of hearing and sight often go unnoticed. Neighborhoods and classrooms harbor bullies and "terrorists" who twist arms, punch noses, choke necks, and trip feet. Schools, parks, playgrounds, homes, and streets may be places where alcohol and drugs are deliberately introduced, foisted upon some, and gladly purchased by others. Kid addicts and alcoholics exist in ample numbers.

Kids' Emotions Can Be Under Siege

Think of the emotional and recognize again that the young can be prey. A kindly granddad baby-sits in order to molest an unsuspecting little girl. A malicious and sick mother browbeats her confused little boy. A sex-addicted dad cons his daughter to believe his love for her includes his instruction in petting and intercourse. A teacher ridicules. A classmate provides and promotes a nasty nickname.

Their Intellect Too

Think of the intellectual and remember the way kids and expectations can be mismatched. The parents and teachers of a child with a learning disability insist he is lazy and defiant. A gifted child is frustrated because neither home nor school recognizes or appreciates her gifts. The shy can be shunned or neglected. Stars are pushed hard and may burn out and fall. Some teachers are determined to disciple their young students into believing that a certain theory is fact or that some fact is a myth.

And Their Social Selves as Well

Think of the social and remember the power your own peers had upon you when you were a little kid or a teen. Some "friends" could get you to cheat and to lie, to break rules and to steal. (Their counterparts are still around.) Others deftly took away your real friends. Some disliked you if you did well on school work and tests. Some belittled you if you made mistakes or got a low grade. Some explained to others that you dressed like a nerd, talked like a nerd, acted like a nerd, and then dramatically deduced that you *were* a nerd. That sort of siege made it plenty apparent that you needed a new wardrobe; a new vocabulary—including some expletives you easily deleted at home; some cool new behaviors that were obnoxious, promiscuous, or dangerous and really dumb.

And Kids' Aesthetical Selves Lay Prey Too

Think of the aesthetical and consider the kind of barrage a kid can encounter because of the arts. A mom insists on flute lessons, even though the child has no aptitude or interest. The siege can go on for years. There are still teachers who expect children to draw a horse, though the students have never been taught to draw a horse, or even how to look closely at horses. These teachers then give a kid a C, or a cutting remark, for the horse he really tried to draw. And then, when these kids draw some great army tanks and missiles on the margins of their math papers, their instructor explodes. Add to that the pressure of singing in the children's choir at church, or the ballet lessons after school, or going to that certain museum. Some very real art-based siege exists for children due to parents' well-intentioned goals and the plans that are set out to meet those goals.

And The Spiritual Is Certain to Be under Siege as Well

Think of the spiritual and try to envision that here too a child can be beset with unreasonable expectation and experience attack. A Christian kid with an unkind, un-Christian parent can face regular and merciless barrages. A child who goes to church regularly may

73

feel strange if his public school teacher and classmates express their disdain for the Lord. The seventh-grade child who bows her head in prayer or sings the chapel hymn may display tremendous courage when the bulk of her Christian school classmates are not praying and not singing. Then there's the Sunday worship service this little kid attends that is often built for adults and ignores him. Yet his parents and pastor expect him to enjoy it, absorb it, and desire more of the same next Sunday. If a teacher does not apply Law and Gospel properly, law-centered instruction can convince a kid that God will love him if he's good, while he knows he isn't. A child may have to endure boring and canned attempts at Gospel instruction because the teacher and the curriculum have been deemed appropriate, even when they aren't.

Clearly Kids Need to Be Protected

Clearly, children do need to be protected in a host of ways. Parents shoulder the lion's share of this responsibility. Others assist. Teachers are in a great position to help. Teachers in Christian schools take on responsibility to shepherd both children and families. Their work includes careful effort to ward off any of the undue negative influences that are part of school life. Teachers can build up each child and family so that they might better cope with the inevitable powerhouse influences that occur in everyday life.

Take TV for Example

Consider the power of television. Parents and teachers have a responsibility to minister to kids regarding the influences of TV. Violent acts and sexual encounters depicted on TV seem to be increasing and becoming increasingly explicit. No time of day or evening is exempt. Cartoons for kids regularly dip into questionable material as they delve into the supernatural and occultic, as well as the violent and sexual.

Television's commercials deserve as much attention as its shows. Children watch them. Often little children pause in their family-room play just for the commercials. The messages are often misleading. The commercial world is on the sell, and it appears to have few scruples regarding its use of whatever voice, scene, word, or concept it can employ to get the selling done.

The Christian teacher watches television too. A regular viewing of TV is a professional task. Watching what is being currently aired is a constant preparation for classroom discussions. Parents and teachers need as much tenacity as TV itself in order to unmask the untruthful, confront the half-truthful, correct the record, and keep television in its rightful place.

TV programming needs vigilant observation and corrective care. It rarely, for example, portrays the family in a positive light. Parents are bumblers. Kids are often shown to be wiser and more effective than their parents. Fathers are particularly inept on TV. Rarely is the sitcom dad in charge and given proper respect. Churches and their staff people are usually presented poorly. Like Dad, they make stupid errors and cart along the same hackneyed, semicomedic roles they've been given over the years.

Children need to know that TV is not real life. There's room for fantasy certainly, but garbage is garbage. Kids and parents need to recognize the difference. Overall we urge our children to watch little, to be selective, to become TV-wise, to turn off junk. We teach them about this important influence and how to prepare for its siege-like intrusion in their lives. We protect them. Television is not always a good friend.

The Good Shepherds of John 10 Protected Their Sheep

Strangers, thieves, and robbers were the enemies Jesus placed into His parable of the good shepherd. His listeners knew well what He meant. A sheepfold needed a high stone wall. Not only were there wolves but dangerous human intruders as well. "The thief comes only to steal and kill and destroy," we read in John 10:10. The Good Shepherd was fully aware of what could happen. He was also pre-pared to fight, to the point of giving His life. The sheep in His charge were not to be stolen. They were not to be killed or destroyed. They were to be protected.

Jesus' parable talks about far more than bruises or a missing tuft of wool. He's talking about souls. There are sheep who may one day miss out on eternal life because of evil people. Salvation is the issue.

But Jesus' instruction is not about gangsters and goons, hit men, or kidnappers. It's not even about thieves. It's about teachers.

Jesus is warning the sheep-fold church of God that some teachers are wolves in sheep's clothing.

Shepherd teachers recognize that false teachers exist everywhere. Any religion that is not of Christ is in the province of false teachers. Consider the huge flocks of people who have been spiritually kidnapped by those who teach Buddhism, Hinduism, Shintoism. Consider the millions led to believe that God gave revelations to his prophet Muhammed that are contained in the Koran. Is there a need to protect one's classroom flock? The global grip of false teaching surely shouts, "Why ask? Can't you see what a worldwide grip the prince of thieves really has?"

Christian teachers recognize that not all false teachers are as obvious as those of an un-Christian religion. Thievery can be hidden and subtle. The cloak may include a building that looks much like a church. The mask may be its name, which states that it is "of Jesus." Its pastors, teachers, and flock members may parade successfully as Christians. But their message misses God's most important ingredient. The great hug isn't there. The Gospel is absent. A shepherding sham draws duped sheep to spiritual death and destruction.

When the Gospel of Jesus Christ as Lord and Savior is not taught as the Bible truth that it is, the sheep find their "salvation" in other means. Salvation is no longer a free gift of God's grace, so the false shepherds provide another means. Most of them point to the good that a person may do as being sufficient. They've managed to convince themselves and their followers that grace can't be free and that love can't be fully accepting without reservation. The great hug has been lost.

A Story to Illustrate How God the Father Isn't

I like the story that Richard Kapfer has written to illustrate the absence of Gospel. It's part of *Helpers of Joy: Applying the Gospel to Life,* (St. Louis: Concordia Publishing House, 1978) pp. 19–20. Read it, remember it, and recognize the "young man." He's one of your relatives. He's a parent of your classroom child. He's your neighbor.

He's one of a long line of sheep who have been stolen from the Lord. Be aware. Beware.

Kapfer writes:

Picture a young man who had just returned home for the summer vacation after having completed his sophomore year at the university. One morning after breakfast his father led him out to the driveway and told him, "I feel that at this point in your life you need to take off from school for a year and discover yourself and the country around you. So, here is a new car, a credit card for its expenses, and money to help support you for the year. You are free to go at any time. I ask just one thing from you, that you always remember that you are my beloved son and that you act like it. I'll write to you, and I hope that you in turn will write to me."

Filled with excitement and anticipation, the young man packed his suitcases and left home. About three hundred miles later, he stopped at a filling station. As he waited for his car to be serviced, a servant of his father, the one that he had remembered as the grouchy one, drove up in a cloud of dust and a squeal of tires. He came up to the man and said: "I'm glad I caught up with you! Do you not know how much your father has done for you?"

"Yes," the son replied. "He has done tremendous things for me. I'm really excited!"

"Then," said the servant, "you ought to show your appreciation. Would it not please him if you would quit acting so irresponsibly and end this foolish journey? After all, look at all that your father has done for you. What are you going to do for him?"

"Well, nothing specific was in my mind," the son replied. "But I love my father, and he loves me. So I felt like just moving along for a year and discovering his love. I'm not sure how I'll express it. But the discovery, I thought, would be fun. I think my father felt the same way."

The servant's face twisted into a pious smile. "Your father, as you know, is very kind—too kind. Would it not please him if you would drive up to the University of Purgatory— a fine school—sell the car, and get busy this summer on your studies for medical school? The money from the sale of the car could be used for something worthy, like for the community that I am starting called The Church of the Perpetuation.

"Furthermore, I am concerned about the attitudes that you are developing. After all, you are your father's son. You should stay away from people who are not of our kind. Avoid the objectionable people. The clothing you wear should reflect the family name. I would suggest browns, grays, and blacks. Perhaps you could sew leather patches on your knees to protect them from the many hours that you will be spending in prayer. And, of course, you will have to be extremely careful of where you go and what you do. In fact, I would suggest that you limit outside contacts to only those that can be trusted. Perhaps I should move in with you to help you in your life."

"But my father gladly gave me the car, the credit card, and the money. His only stipulation was that I act like his son."

"Ah, that is the point! You are not mature enough to know what that means!"

"I thought I did. It seemed so clear, so exciting, so free and beautiful! But now ... "

"You really do need me, my boy!"

"I guess you're right."

So the son lived miserably ever after. Pretty soon he was not sure he knew his father. Even his father's letters did not excite him, and he could not bring himself to explain to his father why he had not taken the trip, for he was ashamed at having taken advantage of his father's generosity. The son no longer felt that his father loved him, and the words of love in his father's letters could no longer convince him. Soon he became afraid of his father. Then he felt guilty about his fear. In time he neither read his father's letters nor wrote to his father. He never went home. It was not very long before he no longer thought of his father, for the thought was too painful for him. The servant could not understand this change in the young man, though otherwise he was an apt pupil. One day the servant washed his hands of the young man and left.

Children are besieged, and the shepherd teacher cannot ignore the harsh realities involved. One way of responding would be to create tough, street-wise kids who have been desensitized and hardened. They'd be quite adult. But that is not the approach to use. Children need to be children. They need to develop. They need nurture. We'll bundle them. We'll gently nurture them physically and socially, emotionally and aesthetically. We'll nurture them intellectually and spiritually.

Skilled Hands to Bundle Those We Shepherd

A Minnesota mother bundles her infant with winter care before heading outdoors. It's cold. There's no need to risk a chill. Her snugly-wrapped child is cushioned and protected. There's an air of confidence about her as she steps into the weather. All will be well.

Keep that picture before you. Change the child's age or change the weather conditions, but keep the picture. Change the scene to the child's first day at preschool and recognize the gentle bundling that is a part of that readiness process. Keep the thoughtful mother as your mentor. It's a helpful image for the shepherding teacher's skilled hands. Let's utilize that picture to look at three special samples of how the bundling applies.

Bundling the Christian Faith

In his book for Christian parents, *Bringing Up Children in the Christian Faith* (Winston Press, 1980), John H. Westerhoff III presents five guidelines for sharing the faith with children from birth through childhood:

We need to tell and retell the biblical story—the stories of faith-together. We need to celebrate our faith and our lives. We need to pray together. We need to listen and talk to each other. We need to perform faithful acts of service and witness together.

The bundling begins. The shepherd's main book is the Bible; the love story between God and people; the story of a covenant made, broken, and renewed, again and again. Jesus and His cross and resurrection is the hub of it all. The shepherd grasps all she can of this awesome love story, determines "to learn it more completely, to understand it more deeply, to possess it more personally,

79

and to live it more fully" (Westerhoff, p. 37). Whether parent or teacher, we need to tell the story as our story, to tell it well, and to tell it often.

The bundling continues. The Bible's stories are of central importance in our lives. We enact them through what we do in worship. We ritualize. It's through our active and shared celebration of what God means to us that we come to know Him. Over and over our worship bundles us as it makes the Lord alive in our hearts, as it communicates God.

The shepherd teacher prepares the child to speak to God and to listen with awe to what He is about to say. She holds this very special book and smiles and speaks of the one called Jesus. The child learns to appreciate and celebrate, to be excited about the big celebration called Baptism and how he can remember it often, even every day. He looks forward with growing anticipation to the celebration of the Lord's Supper. The shepherding teacher deftly brings the story of God into the lives of the children of God.

The bundling includes prayer. Prayer is our response to God's presence. The skilled shepherd begins at that point. His children start their prayer by opening up to God to acknowledge Him, to appreciate His presence. They say their thanks. They tell Him that they love Him. They ask Him, "What do you want us to know, to feel, or to do?" They bring their petitions. The shepherd teacher works hard at making prayer a meaningful part of people's lives. He acts with great care to make prayer the natural and wonderful conversation that it is. He bundles the classroom flock. The Lord's presence prevails and protects.

Bundling includes conversation with children about God. Children ask questions about God. Answering them takes much skill. God's Holy Spirit provides the words. "Who is God?" they ask. "Can I see Him?" They search, "Why did He let Grandpa die? Where is heaven?" They wonder, "How can God love someone that is really bad?" The same questions are sometimes asked by the teacher. The conversation is not idle, speculative chatter. It is part of the bundling. It builds a basis of understanding and an ability to witness. It's very real armor.

The bundling needs real and meaningful acts of service. Children are as much the church as are adults. They have the same responsibilities. Just as the church thrives when its adult members see themselves in ministry, so also classroom Christian learning blossoms when kids get into serving others. Shepherd teachers regularly involve their students in ministry projects. It's one thing to say to children that they can witness to that old lady who lives on their street. It's a whole new proposition to have the class visit the home of an older adult down the block to help her in some way, to bring her cheer,to bring her God's comfort and assurance.

We've given our young some special direction for life if we've instilled in them the notion that they are ministers, a servant people. The "Helpers Chart" is not just fun and not just for getting things done for the teacher.It's life.

Bundling Children's Sexuality

Shepherd teachers worry about their children's sexual development with good cause. There's so much for a boy to sort out when it comes to being male. There's so much for a girl to know and believe as she relates to being female.The wise Christian teacher takes the initiative to work with the principal and parents to develop an annual classroom plan for caring and careful sex education.

It's a quiet curriculum, one that needs to be presented and received as naturally as possible. Lessons are deliberately built into several subjects and spaced throughout the year. The plan makes certain this instruction is neither neglected or overdone. Teaching children about their sexual lives is a truly loving thing to do. We care about kids in a special way as we take the time to select topics and to plan, take the extra pains to prepare lessons and to rehearse presentations, take the risk that some uninformed or ill-intentioned person will cause a stir.

The words *penis* and *vagina* deserve respect and understanding and correct usage. Teachers can learn to comfortably speak these words and establish them as appropriate vocabulary. Children can learn to take in stride a word like *pregnancy* or *sperm,* and to respect and use proper terms related to a healthy understanding of human sexuality.

Even more important are basic concepts: Sex is just one more of God's good gifts to people. God created us to be sexual beings— male and female. We are distinctly different. And alike. Adopting

81

God-pleasing values will bless our sexual choices and challenges.

Lutheran schools have been particularly blessed through the availability of materials that ably assist in the proper handling of sexual information. The six books and attending AV resources that comprise the widely sold *Learning About Sex* series from Concordia Publishing House are excellent. They present a complete and authoritative program of sex education from the Christian perspective.

Christian youngsters can use help at every stage of their sexual development. They need to be shepherded with the understanding that as children they will explore and exploit sexual matters and err as all people do. They can, however, be shepherded with confidence. Honest, responsible instruction works. It takes away awkwardness and embarrassment. It opens doors to healthy and healing communication. There's every reason to believe that we can protect our children from many of the dysfunctional problems, diseases, and dreads that are a part of sexual unhealth. We can count on the blessings that will attend their lives as they relate and date, love and marry, know and grow.

The barrage of sex-hyping advertising, permissive societal habits, and pornographic materials and movies is powerful. The old notion that sex is a dirty subject is powerful. But reverence, respect, and responsibility in the Lord are still more powerful. The siege of sexual misuse and abuse so much a part of American homes and communities is being daily and deftly handled by Christian parents and teachers and pastors.

Building Kids' Self-Esteem

Teachers can deliberately instruct and counsel children so as to build up their self respect. It takes energy and care. It takes competence. It relates to one's own good health. When the shepherd teacher has a wholesome and confident self-esteem, he is able to see and hear what needs to be done for his flock.

Good teachers verbalize their approval and trust. They convey their faith in children. As teachers communicate their belief in kids, the kids believe in themselves as well.

Dr. Herman Glaess of Concordia College in Seward, Nebraska, has helped Christian teachers grow as shepherds of children's self-esteem. One way he effectively did so for me was by sharing the story of the dipper and the bucket. *Each of us is much like a bucket. Each of us has a dipper. As we dip into ourselves in order to fill another's bucket we discover that our own bucket does not go down as we might expect. It goes up. Similarly, as we selfishly dip into someone else's bucket to build up ourselves through some ridicule or cheap-shot sarcasm, we are surprised by this bucket mystery. Our own bucket level goes down instead of up.*

I also recall Dr. Glaess saying that, as a principal, he wished he could daily give each of his teachers a twenty dollar bill. His purpose was to keep his teachers tuned sharply to the important matter of self-esteem. He imagined that every time a teacher's word or action was detrimental to a child's self-worth, the teacher would give up a dollar. He wondered what would be left of the twenty by the end of the day.

A healthy self-image is basic to being a well-adjusted child. The child is comfortable with who she is. She has been well-loved, so she feels worthy of love. She likes herself. It seems quite natural to her that others will like her too. A toddler who repeatedly hears "good girl" ultimately believes in her goodness—a goodness her family and teachers will explain, that grows from Jesus' love. For a healthy selp-image is based on trust in God's word about our image—we are His beloved children. Children for whom He sent His Son to die.

Chuck Swindoll often plugs the importance of self-esteem as he writes and speaks to Christian families and congregations. High self-esteem is not to be confused with a noisy conceit. Swindoll sees it as a quiet sense of self-respect, a feeling of self worth. Because of what Jesus has done for you, you are glad you're you. Conceit is more aptly seen as a whitewash to cover low self-esteem. With a good self-image you don't waste time and energy impressing others. You don't have to; you already know you have value.

A child's view of herself influences her choice of friends, how she gets along with others, the kind of person she'll marry, and the use she makes of her gifts and abilities. It also takes a lot of confidence to be a servant. Self-respect affects a child's creativity (think about artwork), his integrity (think about homework), his stability (think about handling tragedy), and how he lives all parts of his life. There's really no way the shepherd of children can overemphasize self-esteem. It's much like a mainspring that clocks kids for success or failure.

Worms or Butterflies

It is certainly good theology for us to recognize that we are sinful beings and that no good that we might do can earn God's love. But there's much more to the great hug of the Gospel. A child secure in Jesus Christ claims the greatest reason in the world to feel good. His forgiveness is complete. Tucked away in the word *confidence* is the Latin root *fide*. Jesus' love and forgiveness gives us a marvelous affirmation of worth. (Jesus loves *me,* this I know.) In Christ we are butterflies. Martin Luther stressed that Christians are both saints and sinners. Although we are worms with constant bents toward evil, we are nevertheless butterflies and have every reason to believe in what Christ does in and through us as we move forward into life.

Wise Teachers Focus Attention

Focused attention is one of the guiding principles for builders of self-esteem. A teacher is an important person in the eyes of a child. If you think like a child for a moment, you can readily register the thought, "Wow, I must be pretty important if this powerful and busy teacher person takes herself away from her important work to look at me." Eyes meeting eyes, ears obviously hearing, a voice that speaks with acceptance and affirmation—together they help kids see themselves as people of value.

Teachers need the skill to separate a child from a specific action. Calmly addressing a misbehavior as a bad choice is different than declaring the misbehaver a bad person. Self-esteem is bound to suffer if being caught in a lie results in being viewed as a liar. A shepherding teacher describes the unacceptable behavior, tells the child how that action makes her feel, and helps the child describe an appropriate replacement behavior. This respect helps the child feel, "She believes in me. I can be a wiser person next time.I know I can."

Self-Esteem Boosters

Teachers can plan deliberate actions that will boost self-esteem. A faculty sharing session unearths good and practical ideas:

I daily strive to use each child's name in a positive way, connecting it with something helpful and good.

I identify at least one thing in which each of my students excels and use that as a regular conversation topic. A child that is a good swimmer will find me talking to him about swimming. I find value in building on strengths. My child-of-the-week bulletin board is a very positive event for each of my kids. I make sure that pictures, items they treasure, their heroes, their hobbies, and their loved ones become a part of the display.

I take a photograph of each preschooler I visit in August. It, and things that I save during the year, become a part of a scrapbook we build together and give to the parents toward the end of the year.

I involve my children regularly as I put up the artwork they do. As a child helps me select a location for her painting, I affirm her artistry. If she prefers not to display it, I respect her wishes.

Whenever I have my kids do a skit or play, I work hard at assigning parts to really fit well. Then we work at it. Drama is a great way to help children become more confident.

Bastioned

The children we teach are precious. Nothing their parents might bring to school could be of greater value. We will use all the skill we can muster to help these children to be strong and healthy and to prepare them well for the future.

Shepherds not only recognize the enemies of their sheep, they protect the sheep, provide them well-defended positions, and point them to strongholds. Disappointment, defeat, and depression will come. The shepherd of the Lord will stand ready.

God has equipped us. The One who has called us into our work is a bastion Lord, our fortress. He is also our equipper. We have our staff and more. In Ephesians Paul outfits us with a suit of armor,

85

helmet and all. He puts a shield in one hand and a sword in the other. We're equipped.

Paul's picture reminds us that the battle is spiritual and that it is fought in God's strength. We not only *teach* a dependence on God, we *live* it in our teaching and in our shepherding. Our skilled and protecting hands are quick to take up the Bible, the Word of God, the sword of the Spirit. Those same skilled hands are quick to fold. Paul wraps up his armor imagery, "Pray in the Spirit on all occasions with all kinds of prayers and requests. With this in mind, be alert and always keep on praying for all the saints" (Eph. 6:18). We depend on God. Our little saints need all kinds of prayers and requests. They are sieged.

We won't simply bundle the sieged in fluffy blankets. Each will be issued his own little suit of armor. We buckle the belt of truth for each one. Their well-fitted breastplates of righteousness are in place. We have a whole row of helmets, one for each boy and girl. And together we put them on with love and care and prayer. God protects them. They are going to be bastioned well.

Notes

1. James Dobson, *Dr. Dobson Answers Your Questions About Raising Children* (Wheaton, IL: Tyndale House Publishers, Inc., 1986) exemplifies a knowledgeable and skillful Christian author's concerted effort to provide answers regarding discipline, respect, and parental leadership on the principles that have come through the Judeo-Christian traditions. In the book's introduction Dobson says "My task has been merely to report what I believe to be the prescription of the Creator Himself."
2. *Time* (Oct. 8, 1990) has a large soulful-eyed picture of the face of a little girl on its cover. Next to it in large yellow words is the question, "Do We Care About Our Kids?" Below those words in bold white letters on black background the cover announces "The sorry plight of America's most disadvantaged minority: its children." The cover story headline on page 42 reads "Shameful Bequests to the Next Generation." Its subhead explains further: America's legacy to its young people includes bad schools, poor health care, deadly addictions, crushing debts—and utter indifference.
3. Richard Kapfer, *Helpers of Joy: Applying the Gospel to Life* (St. Louis: Concordia Publishing House, 1978).
4. David Elkind, *The Hurried Child: Growing Up Too Fast Too Soon* (Reading: Addison-Wesley, 1981) broke a lot of ground on behalf of the unique burdens we have placed upon children. Its insight and advice is still applicable. Hurried children continue to make up a large portion of the troubled children seen by

clinicians today; they constitute many of the young people experiencing school failures, those involved in delinquency and drugs,and those who commit suicide. Valuable book for teachers who care about children.

5. John H. Westerhoff III, *Bringing Up Children in the Christian Faith* (Minneapolis: Winston Press, 1980) is not meant to be an expert's guide to the right way to bring up children in the Christian faith. It is rather a reflective sharing of the struggles involved in being a faithful Christian parent (teacher), a testimony to the faith we share in the grace of God—grace that we need, our children need.

6. *Learning About Sex: A Series for the Christian Family* (St. Louis: Concordia Publishing House, 1988) is a set of six books and five videos that provide a biblically-based perspective on sex and sexuality. Every Christian teacher ought to periodically view the whole video package (age 3–teen) to re-establish sexuality as a gift from God that can be taught and learned, and that can bring about greater responsibility and self-esteem in children's lives.

7. Lenore Buth, *How to Talk Confidently with Your Child About Sex* (St. Louis: Concordia Publishing House, 1988) is the outstanding companion piece for the above series, 160 pages.

8. Charles R. Swindoll *Growing Wise in Family Life* (Portland: Multnomah Press, 1988) includes Chapter 7 (pp. 131–149) which is titled"Affirmation: Enhancing Esteem."

9. The theory of "The Dipper and the Bucket" was formulated by Donald Clifton, the president of Selection Research Associates. In it Clifton suggests that we all carry an invisible bucket that determines how we feel about ourselves. Others are constantly filling or lowering our bucket through their words and actions. Kenneth Erickson describes the theory further in *The Power of Praise* (St. Louis: Concordia Publishing House, 1984), pp. 21–22.

CHAPTER 8

Watching over the Flock

Boring, But You'll Have Them Based and Blessed

"And there were shepherds living out in the fields nearby, keeping watch over their flocks at night" (Luke 2:8).

It had to be a boring business, this work of a shepherd. Not enough that this job took you out of your house and away from family, that it called for an acceptance of simple food, primitive lodging, and wearing clothes weeks between washings. Not enough that you often felt lonely and shortchanged. There was more, and it had to do with large blocks of the job's time. It was pretty boring. Shepherding demanded a diligence amidst the routine. Keeping watch over sheep, like keeping watch over anything, is bound to be a wearisome and monotonous task.

The Bethlehem bunch was a rare exception. They had an indescribably wonderful break from their boredom. It was enough to scare you out of your wits. Recall that it was night. Imagine yourself dozing near the warmth of a fire. And then . . . an angel. Never before and never again, but there was no mistake. It was an angel! Unbelievable. Impossible, but there it was. And it spoke. The splendent apparition had an equally awesome message. We've revelled in it since. "Today in the town of David a Savior has been born to you; He is Christ the Lord." And then followed the fireworks. A sky-lighting flurry of grandeur and majesty. Gobs of angels. What a spectacle! What a sound! What a song!

The trips followed. They hustled off to the manger to find Mary and Joseph and the baby. It was true. Mary undoubtedly confirmed it. Joseph likely filled in the pieces. God had indeed decided on this time and this place to send His Son. Wow, what news! What an experience to savor and share. People were amazed at what these shepherds had to say. Who knows how many whom they told also sought out the manger to see Jesus? Who can tell how much it warmed the hearts of the hearers to have this word of God's great messianic hug.

Christian teachers identify well with the shepherds as they joy in sharing the news of Christ's birth. It's great to kneel at the manger, to worship there in the context of the cross, and to head away to tell of God's marvels. But being a teacher, like being a shepherd, certainly calls for boring tasks as well.

There's plenty in the task of teaching that is tied up in tedium. Supervising children can be dreary and dull at times. Much of evaluation is an irksome and fatiguing process. Repetition may be the mother of learning, but it also is often a real drag.

But just as there were no apologies for shepherds having to watch over their sheep, there are no apologies for teachers. Overseeing children and their work and their lives is a vital part of the work. Out of weeks and months of watching come wonderful inspirations. Something clicks. A veritable angel descends. Ah-ha, this is what I must do tomorrow to get this group to the manger. Ah-ha, now I know just what to say to get Shareena's dad to the cross. Ah-ha, I have it. This is what my class will sing next month at the 11:00 service. Ah-ha, beautiful! This is how Jorge will hear the Gospel.

You see, watching over the flock may be boring, but it is also a big part of knowing what's going on. Through the day-in-and-day-out of being together and working with one another we figure out this flock, we come to anticipate the needs of the sheep, we know them. Out of basic understandings come great blessings. So much of our spiritual ministry will grow legs while we are watching over the flock. Soon the ministry will get underway. We'll be off and running.

Home Visits Provide Beginning Bases

It happened over 30 years ago, but I still remember the home visits I made on my fourth and fifth graders just prior to my first year in teaching. I see the streets and the homes. I recall where I sat. I see the parent or parents. I see a child.

I see John and his searching, accepting eyes. He's going to be a great learner. (He was.) I see Dennis. He's all over the living room.

His mother has no control and neither does Dennis. (I still don't know what he did with my turtle.) I see Janice and her smiling, thoughtful parents. What saints, all three of them. I see Victor. His mom is terribly overprotective. I knew he'd be unable to catch a ball or hold a bat. (He couldn't.) I also knew I'd bring him great joy in teaching him how to hit. (I did.) I see Lotte and her immigrant mom, and I remember seeing much of myself in this tall, gifted girl.

And I see Diane. She's at her kitchen table and so am I. So is her dad. We're sitting in their farmhouse west of town. Diane's mom is busily canning vegetables as we talk. Her eyes are sad. Unhappiness dwells in this house. I feel that, and I feel sorry for Diane. I'm pretty certain that her dad is an alcoholic. I know that Diane has a great mom, a loving and dedicated parent, but I also can see that Diane will often be far behind in her lessons. I was right on all counts. I know that I ministered to Diane in some special ways. When her homework wasn't finished, or when she fell asleep in class, or when her eyes were red from crying, I knew how to minister to her.

What a blessing to begin a base of information by visiting a child's family. What further blessing as over the years I became more skilled in the family-visiting process and could make the most of questions and answers, observations, and collection of family data.

Yes, visiting 30 or 40 homes was a tedious process. Boring it wasn't, but it was a demanding chore to complete. The rewards, however, were great. My work was not teaching math and science. My work was teaching children. The shepherding had begun.

There's a Whole Lot More to Reporting Kids' Progress than Putting Letter Grades in Little Boxes

Of all the drearisome tasks in which the teacher must engage, none compares with doing report cards. It's a dedication to myth that a teacher can actually use A, B, C, D, and F to accurately sum up a quarter of lessons, homework, projects, and tests in eight or nine subjects for 25 kids. Each of those 25 students began the quarter in a different place, and each has a different level of capability.

How to fairly report the 44-day progress for a child of low ability, or for one who has a learning disability, is another part of an impossibly difficult task. Both may be working very hard. Both may

90

be making great strides, but still be scoring very poorly on cross-classroom tests. In the meantime, a gifted student may be registering little actual progress, even though he passes test after test with near-perfect scores. It's a process fraught with difficulty, especially since most parents and children view report cards as tools for reward and punishment. Sadly, many teachers do too.

Reporting to parents involves evaluation and communication. Parents need to be well-informed to be good partners. Putting together valid observations takes much care and a lot of work. Wise teachers choose words carefully and well. Parents and children differ and the shepherding teacher learns to approach them individually, offering the evaluation, advice, and support that will help the most.

Parent-Teacher Conferences

Nothing is more valuable in parent-teacher communications than a well-prepared conference. It is most effective when parents prepare as well. They, too, have observations to share and can jot down questions to be asked.

The shepherding teacher begins the conference with prayer, one that includes thanks to the Lord for the wonderful gift He has given in this child, and one that seeks God's blessing on relationships with child and parents.

Part of the conference focuses on the child's spiritual growth. The teacher shares specific examples related to the child's witness of faith. Saving examples of written paragraphs, poems, prayers, and Christian art can be very helpful in this sharing. Jotting a note when the child demonstrated a caring action is another powerful help. The shepherd teacher is curious about how things are going at home for the child in terms of prayer and worship, and in other examples of Christian faith in action. Church and Sunday school attendance can be discussed and encouraged.

Choosing the right words takes skill. A teacher grows in her ability to plan and prepare, to make notes and to speak with parents. A teacher practices good eye contact, sincerity, and honesty in her presentation. Improvement comes with each conference.

Cogent Comments Convince and Compel

Being able to minister well to kids through written comments is an important skill. It takes work. It takes care. Children and parents appreciate that work and care. Writing a brief sentence of appreciation atop a homework assignment is far superior to a letter grade or stamped smiley face. It's a thoughtful and positive reflection that says, "I really know and understand you. I appreciate your effort. I have your best interest in mind as I give you work to do, and as I evaluate it with care."

Part of the skill in writing worthwhile comments for kids is to follow up a general statement with a specific example. "Great work!" is a nice reward. "Great work . . . I especially enjoyed your third paragraph. Good choice of words," demonstrates thoroughness and interest. "Poor Work!" may motivate better work next time, but "Ooops, it looks like you need to multiply more carefully," may be a more helpful and positive motivator. Humor and hallelujahs motivate. Criticism and caustic remarks will not. We need only ask ourselves how we'd react under similar circumstances. Well-chosen words keep the ball rolling. Positive comments give our students' work the regard and honor it deserves.

Prayer Takes Skill Too

The shepherd teacher works at prayer. It, too, has its skill side and requires thought, preparation, and practice. Prayer can be reverent and earnest or it can be lost in routine, irrelevance, and habit. The one who leads a group in prayer or calls the shots for what praying a group does has a major responsibility. Prayer realizes God's presence. We bow heads and fold hands to help register the devout respect and sincere devotion we feel in our hearts.

There's a personal and private side to the shepherd's work of watching over the flock in prayer. These children can be daily brought to the Lord's lap or not. Their special needs can become patient petitions or forgotten issues. Their families can grow stronger through the shepherd's fervent prayer or can be less than they might be due to prayer disregard and disuse. The caring and watchful shepherd teacher strives to do the job well, to daily uphold, surround, and strengthen his children in the prayer he brings. It may be his most important work.

How does it get done? How does it get done well? What can we learn from those who have struggled with these questions? Listen as some shepherd teachers share about prayer and getting it done.

Mr. P: I like to use a daily prayer card. As I start a school year, I make out seven cards, one for each day of the week. I divide my students' names into seven groups and write them on the cards. I try to pray each day for one group of children, each by name. I add other people to these lists, for example, the four kids whom I serve as Baptism sponsor.

Miss G: Before I leave my classroom at the end of the day I look over the empty desks and think about the children and their needs. I ask the Lord to watch over them and to keep them close to Himself. It's a kind of benediction that I've come to make up each day.

Miss S: How do I get it done? Not too well, I'm afraid. Surprisingly, I often forget to pray for them for days. I do, however, jot down the names of people in my plan book for whom I'm praying. My students and families with special needs do get prayed for. I tend to pray each morning for the class as a whole as I ask the Lord to bless my work in the day ahead.

Mrs. R: Two meaningful things come to mind. As I plan my devotions and Christian learning class for the day, I think about my children and ask the Holy Spirit to bless my teaching of the Word. I often think of individual children as I pray. The other special thing is that I try to pray for my class as part of my worship in church on Sunday. I try to remember kids and their parents who have special needs. I ask God to be with those who made it to church and pray that He would bless their worship and their faith. Then I also ask Him to be with those who didn't make it to church. I pray that He would watch over their spiritual lives and keep them from spiritual harm or danger.

Mr. B: Along with trying to pray for my students on a regular basis I also try to get others to do so. I try to kind of multiply my prayers for my kids by involving others whenever I can.

My wife is a big help, for example. She likes to pray for others. I bring children by name to her whom I'd like her to include in her prayers. I ask our pastors and other teachers to pray for any of my kids with special needs. I definitely get my kids to pray for one another. Sometimes I think that's the best kind, one child earnestly praying for another. When someone's absent from school, the rest of us pray for that person. I guess I'm kind of a prayer-beggar now that I think about it. I try to scrounge up prayers for my kids whenever I can. It's part of my looking out for them.

Mrs. S: I try to make a prayer list each day. It's odd, but it's usually on vacation days or weekends that I forget, even though I have the time. Anyway, my list is whoever comes to mind, not just children and not just those in some dramatic need. It really helps to write it down. Many times the list includes names from the day before. I try to pray for specific things for each person on the list, but I also just commend the whole list to God's care. He knows their needs, and I know that He cares for each one.

Kids Go to Hospitals Too

When children are injured in an accident or homebound or hospitalized, a shepherd teacher swings into special action. The teacher not only prays, but focuses on that child and family with spiritual care, with smiles, with conversation, with mail from the class, with ideas that make a hospital stay less of a drudge.

Hospital visits take careful time management and sometimes the sacrifice of other activities. Each visit is worth the time and effort it takes.

When a parent or other family member is in the hospital room during a visit, you get to minister to those persons as well. As a shepherd teacher your hospital mission includes sharing God's concern. You do so in a natural way. You can gently involve others by asking them to describe an occasion when they were very glad that the Lord was with them. You might hold hands for prayer. It's a perfect way to involve everyone, even hospital roommates and friends and families.

A hospital visit provides a valuable occasion to help children and families recognize that it was not God's plan that they be hurt or sick. It was not God's doing, or even His idea, that a drunk driver would lose control of his automobile and strike this child as she was riding her bike along the sidewalk. The accident occurred as a result of a world mired in sin and the act of a careless person.

We emphasize the presence of God. He is by our side. He assures us that regardless of the duration or outcome of a hospital stay, He will be there and help us cope with the difficulties and handle our fears and our worries. He will also be with those on the hospital staff. That's part of the picture of God's presence. His ministering people are everywhere, also in hospitals.

Most pastors become quite skilled in their ability to make the spiritual most of a hospital or homebound call. Doing some visits to shut-ins or hospitalized members with one's pastor provides good training. Consider asking your pastor to train the teachers on your staff and give you helpful tips regarding this kind of ministry.

Our Shepherd Watch Becomes Our Way

The classroom shepherd's antennae are always up. She needs to know what's going on in the life of her flock. Anticipating needs is important. Good teachers manage to spot things that are out of kilter.

It took sixth-grade teacher Mr. B. just a short while to realize that a magazine being covertly passed across the aisle was an unwelcome classroom addition. In moments he quietly intercepted the porn-laced publication and ministered to those involved. He didn't begin an all classroom harangue, but all of his flock quickly sensed the import of his action. A serious matter had occurred, and it had been quickly detected and appropriately handled. It was like the scoutmaster who spots a black widow spider near one scout's tent and quietly squashes the intruder with his boot.

The classroom takes on the character of the shepherd. The teacher sets the tone. This is particularly good if the tone is set from the shepherd's heart. The climate of the room becomes one of care and compassion, of firmness with a gentle touch.

A school takes on the character of its combined classroom shepherds. Six severe and business-like teachers with a penchant for hard-nosed rules can soon establish an atmosphere that exudes a law-based and little-joy attitude for their school. Just as easily, one watchful shepherd can take note of this imbalance, bring it to the attention of the other five, and with their help return the climate to good health.

Each Christian school shepherd helps watch over the whole school in order to keep its overall tone as Gospel-like as possible, as positive and caring as one might expect it to be. Each has the responsibility to be alert to what can get in the way of shepherd ministry, harm it, or destroy its effectiveness.

A school, for example, with a brusque principal and curt office secretary may well collect tuition dollars on time, but also drive away parents. Yes, school has its business side, but those who shepherd it must always recognize the value of the individual, precious souls whom God leads into the fold. Each teacher is aware of what each part of the school's program can do to build Christian community or tear it apart.

As stated in a marvelous monograph called *"The School as a Caring Community"* (Lutheran Education Association, 1986), school can be a downer. "Many children and youth of every age, community, and economic level experience the daily pain of school—of failed tests, peer rejection, impossible-to-reach expectations of parents and teachers and the like." Shepherd teachers are on the watch for negative experiences.

Pain at school is not necessarily limited to students. The monograph notes that "teachers also experience the pain of broken relationships. The problem of classroom discipline, pressure from supervisors, hassling from disgruntled parents, etc., all contribute to teacher dissatisfaction, burnout, and dropout."

Shepherd teachers watch out for one another and for their administrators, their pastors and other congregational staff. Conflicting and clashing ministry approaches, attitudes, and actions must be spotted, exposed, and managed. Breakdowns are no fun. Broken relationships are just like collapsed bridges. The detours that ensue spell ineffectiveness, inconvenience, and unhappiness. The school community suffers. Children and families get less care and less ministry. How vital it is for all who are church workers to recognize the power they have in Christ to be at watch, to be caring and forgiving, to be courageous in speaking and intervening in loving ways, to be at prayer.

I Will Place Shepherds over Them

We recall the Lord's declaration regarding the people of Judah in Jer. 23:4. "I will place shepherds over them who will tend them, and they will no longer be afraid or terrified, nor will any be missing." God's will is clear. Sheep-tending calls shepherds to keep the flock calm and untroubled, to be alert to circumstances that cause fear or terror. The shepherd teacher often encounters children and adults who are afraid and terrified. May it never be the case that the cause of their fright and alarm comes from the school community.

Classroom shepherds constantly draw on the One who is always alert and never tiring. Our great God is with us, the One whom the psalmist so aptly describes in Ps. 121:3–4: "He who watches over you will not slumber; indeed He who watches over Israel will neither slumber nor sleep." The Lord of all creation is our guardian shepherd in every way.

Classroom shepherds can't be always alert and untiring, but each can point to and represent the One who is that way. Each can rely on God's power and presence to get the wearisome watching job done. It's a big part of shepherding.

Notes

Robert J. L. Zimmer and Phyllis N. Kersten, *The School as a Caring Community* was published by the Lutheran Education Association, River Forest, Illinois as the Winter 1986, vol. 11:2, publication of the Lutheran Education Association Monograph Series.

CHAPTER 9
Leading the Flock

Brought, Built Up, and Bringers-to-Be

Shepherds lead. It's the classic task of shepherds. The scriptural favorite of shepherding imagery, Psalm 23, sketches the picture.

Leading gets the sheep from pen to pasture. The psalmist leads his company to "lie down in green pastures." Leadership implies improvement. The sheep have a better place to eat, to feed, and to relax.

The leading continues. The shepherd brings the flock to quiet waters. Water is as vital as food.

Leaders know about those being led. They understand needs. They bring balance to work and play.

Leaders think on behalf of those being led. The flock needs to be built up. When the charges are children, the drama escalates. The shepherd teacher realizes that each child is simply a budding leader, another bringer-to-be. Leadership is as much a little-kid proposition as it is one for a teen or an adult.

See It in Rebecca at the Lamb's Lot

For a number of years my administrative ministry included the joyous task of regularly stopping by our parish preschool, the Lamb's Lot. It's fun to observe little children. They're busy. Absorbed. Free. They develop before your very eyes, like a photographer's time-lapse study of a budding flower.

A little child changes daily. As I write, Rebecca is "three going on six." She's a lamb-and-a-half, a little kid with a lot of charisma. Her bright and alert eyes register quick greeting. They are widely intent upon all that is happening around her. Life is great! I must capture all of it I can, says Rebecca's countenance as she gives herself to yet another facet of her preschool day. I'm involved in a very busy and important day.

Rebecca is gifted. And she's not only blessed with beaucoup capability. Rebecca's been gifted with two great parents who raise her with skill and love, patience and care. Susan and John talk to Rebecca a lot. They read to her all the time. So does Sarah, her big sister, a third grader. Rebecca has been blessed with a major head start in communication. What a leadership help that is. Her family plays with her, prizes her, teaches her about Jesus and God's world, and about church and family. Rebecca is miles ahead, so advanced one might ask, "Who needs a shepherding preschool?"

Rebecca does. This little dynamo, brimming with promise and personality, needs exactly that—and it's great to watch it working. Her shepherd squad at the Lamb's Lot is alert. The trio of teachers who team to cover the 30 Tuesday-Thursday three-year-olds all understand and appreciate this heads-up little girl.

While Rebecca stands out clearly as an example of a little child who is a leader now, and certainly a leader-to-be, all children need to be viewed in a similar light. Each is so different from the next, yet each is going to be involved throughout life in a variety of leadership tasks. Some will have huge responsibilities we'd never have imagined. The collective future possibilities for a flock are vast, inestimable in number and value, wondrous to imagine when harnessed for the Lord.

Leadership Touches So Much

Be mindful as a classroom teacher of how much leadership means for people day in and day out. I lead my life. You lead yours. My wife and I lead our family. You (and your spouse) lead yours. Every family in your neighborhood depends on its built-in leadership.

Leadership is truly all around us. City officials and business managers lead. Leadership is needed at the hospital, baseball stadium, mouse trap factory, the company that develops and distributes computer software, the massive complex that manufactures automobiles.

Leadership enters every endeavor. It makes a difference. Its absence signals problems. Its proper presence makes things hum and purr.

Churches Need a Lot of It

The church needs leadership from both staff and membership. There's much to do. Worship to lead. Prayers to lead. Choirs to lead. Every-member visitations to lead. Meetings that need shepherding, planning retreats need to be organized and led. Boards, councils, and committees call for leadership. A congregation planting a daughter congregation gives away leadership, as does the church that draws its community into a plan to care for the homeless, the poor, and those struck down by tragedy. *Think of the many ways we'll need our Rebeccas to help.*

All church education requires successful leadership. Sunday schools, elementary schools, day care centers and preschools, vacation Bible school and summer day camp need that director or principal, superintendent or co-superintendent who gives extra hours, uses special skills, and envisions what the program should be when it's at its best. Effective administrators need to be good leaders. *Perhaps Rebecca will be a principal of a Christian day school.*

Leadership Involves Many Things

Effective leadership involves skills and attitudes, knowledge, habits, and conduct. Leading is a complex business, and topnotch leaders are not simply born that way.

Leadership is learned. Leadership is earned. And, finally, leadership is presented. It's bestowed upon those who have demonstrated certain necessary ingredients.

Lesser leaderships precede significant leaderships. A long chain of leadership links begin with Rebecca the preschooler and reach to Dr. Rebecca, the president of her college, of her company, of her country.

What skills will she need? What should we be preparing her to do? How can we help the children we teach and nurture become the effective leaders of tomorrow? Consider these skills:

Rebecca's Leadership Skills List

1. *Goal-setting skills that identify direction and achieve objectives.* Rebecca will need techniques to help her focus on the future and to measure progress. Planning strategies will streamline her

work and multiply what she and her staff get done.

2. *Decision-making strategies that eliminate doubt and delay.* She'll need to move from the problem to the solution calmly and logically. Analysis worksheets and priority grids and reaching consensus will help her maximize her peoples' potential.

3. *Team-building dynamics to boost morale and performance.* She'll need to not only be a team person, but know how to skillfully construct, develop, and motivate the team she leads. Conflicting personalities and attitudes will not deter her team from being united and effective. She'll develop interaction techniques that will help create new and constructive stepping stones.

4. *Develop awareness of her organization's "culture" and how it works.* She'll value the delineation of roles and responsibilities. She'll understand how the politics involved in her workplace affect her and how she should affect them.

5. *Financial and stewardship skills to forecast and manage well.* She'll understand budgets and the rigorous and dynamic process involved in using them well. Her personnel will be involved and properly rewarded and recognized.

6. *Effective idea communication to reinforce her credibility.* Good listening and presentation skills will greatly help her do her work. Recognizing key psychological elements will maximize the impact of her written communication.

The Art of Leadership

Leadership is not all that easy to explain. I was recently asked to make a three-hour presentation on leadership for a conference of Christian day school principals. That was a challenge. Leadership is a vital topic for anyone who has been put in charge of others, whether a corporation or a class of third graders. The bottom line for leadership is that those being led reach their full potential. That's quite a commission. It requires a masterful kind of shepherding.

Three basic types of shepherding exist. One leader-shepherd's approach sees itself in being way out ahead of the flock. It sets the pace, and never mind that the sheep are way behind, their needs not being met. It's their job to keep up.

A second view imagines the shepherd right behind the flock,

beating the ignorant, unheedful, lazy sheep with a rod to force them on their way.

A shepherd, however, is neither a scout nor a cowboy. Instead, he is properly in the midst of the flock, walking in what they walk and stepping in what they step. The shepherd is a servant as well as a leader, staying lovingly in touch with each of the sheep.

Shepherding teachers put the growth and development of children ahead of their homework tasks, test results, and their own needs as teachers. They work at building children up.

It's Like Coaching

Coaching a grade school basketball team comes to mind as a parallel. The coach needs to know about children and care for those on her team. She's taken time to equip them well, to school them with fundamentals, and to get them into good condition. She has also practiced with them diligently so that they can work together as a team.

And while she strives for her team to play well and to work to win, she'll never shout her disappointment across the game floor when a player makes that terrible pass or takes a very bad shot. (That's not serving. It's not building.) She'll also avoid that demeaning word to the kid who has just committed that "stupid" foul. (Her players' feelings and dignity are more important.) It's her goal that the players will feel good about the game as well as themselves.

That kind of coaching cares about kids. It's sound leadership. It demonstrates that relationships count more than scores and records.

A Book That's on Track

An excellent and applicable book has been written about leadership. The author is Max De Pree, an executive officer in one of America's top businesses. *Leadership Is an Art* describes a people-first style of management begun years ago by his father, D. J. De Pree, and the great success the company and its employees have enjoyed for more than 60 years. While the book is about business leadership, its ideas about organizational leadership are highly appropriate for church and school ministries.

The De Pree concept of leadership is based on Jesus' teaching in Luke 22. The Gospel writer quotes Jesus:

The kings of the Gentiles lord it over them; and those who exercise authority over them call themselves Benefactors. But you are not to be like that. Instead, the greatest among you should be like the youngest, and the one who rules like the one who serves. For who is greater, the one who is at the table or the one who serves? Is it not the one who is at the table? But I am among you as one who serves (Luke 22:25–27).

Jesus was quelling His disciples' dispute over which of them was the greatest. He was also conferring upon them His kingdom, an upside-down kingdom in the world's perspective. The One in charge is servant to those in His charge.

De Pree's Jesus-led views provide a special way of thinking about people. The artful leader, De Pree believes, is a steward of the gifts, abilities, and potential of everyone in his company. "People are the heart and spirit of all that counts. Without people, there is no need for leaders" (p. 13). "Leaders are also responsible for future leadership. They need to identify, develop, and nurture future leaders" (p. 14). "Leaders owe a certain maturity" to their people. "Maturity as expressed in a sense of self-worth, a sense of belonging, a sense of expectancy, a sense of responsibility, a sense of accountability, and a sense of equality" (pp. 15–16).

Do you hear what De Pree's focus is? People come first, not the tasks they accomplish. Would that all who spiritually shepherd might have as great a commitment to those the Lord has given them to lead.

As One's Flock Is on the Way to Heaven

The classroom flock makes many stops, but it is bound for the sheepfold that is eternal. Rebecca and her lamb-like buddies are to be in heaven one day. The shepherd leader *has* to know that, must recognize fully where her flock is headed.

The flock needs to be properly fed along the way. Spiritual nurture is necessary for faith to grow and develop. We teach the Word of God to keep each sheep close to God.

The trip is not an aimless meandering on the way to heaven. The sheep and shepherd have purpose along the way. There's ministry on every side. So Paul describes it in the last three chapters of Ephesians. God looks for His children of every age to be constantly in service to those around them.

Each child is to be skillfully and intentionally immersed in the notion that every person of the church is a minister. Each is to be a life-long giver. At the same time, each one must be taught to receive, to be one to whom ministry comes, for every person is also a life-long receiver. God leads His people to a wonderful and significant balance. We give and receive. That's life. That's what ministry is all about. *That's what we are leading Rebecca to understand and apply.*

God's design calls us to help one another and to forgive one another. He asks us to encourage one another. It's all part of His saint-equipping plan, a mutual ministry that gets the flock where it needs to go. Viewing one's classroom as a little congregation of ministers helps it happen.

Viewing the classroom as a happy and healthy little parish is helpful. It's bound to flourish best when the teacher is herself a parish-bonded, congregation-wise person who knows a lot about what makes a good church tick. The effective shepherd leader is apt to be the one who identifies strongly with his own congregation, is well aware of parish pains and joys. He's a person who is particularly involved in Sunday's worship and in its education and fellowship.

A valuable little paperback that describes nicely the kind of scriptural and caring congregation the leader teacher might envision is Susan B. Lidum's *Church Family Ministry: Changing Loneliness to Fellowship in the Church.* It's a rich and perceptive resource for the Christian educator, one that points to parish effectiveness through members ministering to each other.

As the flock moves on toward heaven it also grows in number. It is naturally in mission as well as ministry. The leader shepherd is constantly equipping his children to witness and proclaim. Outreach is the flock's great commission. The journey to heaven calls for inclusive thinking. No one is to be left out. No one is too poor or too rich to be targeted for God. No one's religious background should bar him from hearing the gospel of Jesus Christ. It's an awesome task to reach all people for God, but the Spirit of God shepherds the church for the task.

During all the ministry-and-mission trek to heaven, God offers a strengthening hug for all who shepherd. The shepherd is not left to his own devices, not devoid of help. Quite the opposite says the word of the Gospel hug. While one leads, one is led. God the Holy Spirit not only embodies that hug, but also leads us as we lead others to Christ.

Jesus Christ, the Good Shepherd, earned us eternal life regardless of the consequences to Himself. He reached out and brought in the lost sheep. He silently and dutifully walked to the cross to be slaughtered as the Lamb of God. In the hug of forgiveness won there, He brings us scattered sheep from the thickets, takes us in His arms, equips us in the Holy Spirit.

Those *brought* to the Lord are gifted with a great and deep confidence in Him. Those brought to Him are brought to be *built up,* even as lambs are to be imagined as *bringers-to-be.* The confidence grows and extends. The led lambs will shepherd too. They will bring others.

Notes

1. Max De Pree, *Leadership Is an Art* (New York: Dell Publishing, 1989) provides a perceptive and personal appreciation of the obligations facing those who play leadership roles in hierarchical organizations.
2. Susan B. Lidums, *Church Family Ministry: Changing Loneliness to Fellowship in the Church* (St. Louis: Concordia Publishing House, 1985) presents the promise that one of the most effective ways to build a vibrant, caring congregation is through members ministering to each other. That's also true for the classroom.

CHAPTER 10

Speaking to the Flock

Brightened, Bound-Up, and Bridged

People talk to animals. Whether a puppy or canary, guinea pig or kitten, the family's pet is given a name, given special care and conversational status. The dairy farmer, too, knows Daisy and each of her Holstein sisters and greets them fondly at morning milking. The trainer speaks to her dolphins and they smile and respond.

I learned something about that sort of thing one college summer while working on a farm near my central Alberta home. That July I became thoroughly acquainted with Duke and Ole, a team of huge work horses. Spirited and responsive, Duke needed calm and steady control, while laidback and pasture-minded Ole required strong demands and discipline. What a pair! What work! But those hot, endless days of haying rough virgin prairie became easier as Duke and Ole listened to me and became a team. Gradually my words began to count. Understanding meshed with food, water, and care, and soon my voice established an upper hand, and we got the cutting and raking done.

Making words count with animals was important to the Palestinian shepherd of Jesus' John 10 parable. After unbracing the gate the shepherd spoke. Jesus put it simply, "And the sheep listen to his voice. He calls his own sheep by name and leads them out" (v. 3).

I don't picture that parable as a Duke and Ole deal. The pleading and shouting isn't there. No reins. No whip. Just a voice and sheep and ears perk up.

Jesus describes a calm scene. It's an everyday procedure. It's like taking the roll in class. The shepherd raises his voice in a call well-known to the sheep and they respond. He speaks their names.

Jesus' story makes its case. Sheep get to know their shepherd.

It's not really the words that matter, but the one who speaks them. It's a relationship. The shepherd leads. The sheep follow. The shepherd and the sheep know one another. The voice counts because the relationship counts. Jesus says it this way: "He calls his own sheep by name and leads them out. When he has brought out all his own, he goes on ahead of them, and his sheep follow him because they know his voice" (vv. 3b–4)

His. His sheep. His voice. His sheep follow Him because they know His voice.

That's the way it is with a parish pastor. The people of a congregation gradually get to know this person they have called to be their shepherd. From that first sermon on they begin to relate to a person. Those afterservice handshakes and smiles welcome new ties. Through classes and conversations and meals and meetings the relationship grows. Through counsel and prayer the bonds cement.

So when, by chance, the pastor meets a church member family in the aisle of the supermarket, there's a spark of joy. A voice greets them and it's mild and gentle. It's just a little chat time next to the cereal boxes, but the family loves it. Each feels honored to be called by name and to be given a little slice of the conversational pie. As the grocery carts begin to stir, the shepherd asks if they'll be in church tomorrow. They smile and decide yes. This pastor person loves them. They are fully confident in his words and actions. They're glad to be a part of his flock. Meeting him has been like getting a hug. Listening to him in church is like getting a hug from God.

And that's the way it is with a shepherd teacher. Her voice counts. Her greeting matters. On school day number one she meets Kyrene at the classroom door and smiles and leads her to a desk that is just right for Kyrene. It has a little sign on the front of it. "God loves Kyrene," it says. "You'll like it here a lot, Kyrene," says the teacher.

The skill of it all becomes clear as you step back and watch things develop. The shepherd teacher is speaking in order to disciple. Kyrene will soon discover that this teacher person is a leader and one who expects her to follow. This following is taking place all day long. There's a call to worship. There's an invitation to listen to a story from God's Word. There are directions to fold hands. Shortly, there may be instruction on how to use the manual pencil sharpener and then the electric one. There's talk about rules. There are praise words to hear about last year's class, a group that learned to take out its math books promptly, put them in the same corner of the desk and not open them at all until asked to do so. Follow. Follow. Follow.

Kyrene listens and learns to follow.

The shepherd teacher speaks and gets things done. He knows that his skillful use of language carries power. He understands that his words continually motivate his students to follow, to work. He is strategically aware that a tremendous amount of work must be done by this classroom flock. These kids are not here just to watch him work or to be entertained by his puppets and posters. They're here to work. At the end of the day they'll be tired because they've been at work all day.

Effective teachers use language that motivates, that disciplines, that gets things done. Kyrene wants to follow and to listen and to learn. Kyrene doesn't realize it, but her teacher has already worked hard and long at the business of speaking effectively. It began with her education professors who pointed out research finding that the typical teacher does 80 percent of all the talking in the classroom. "It'll be that, and more, as you begin," they warned. "You'll have to learn how to get your kids to do more of the talking," they exhorted. "And the skill and wisdom of speaking much less," they added.

Experience taught Kyrene's teacher a lot about speaking. On the first day of her first school year, for example, she learned that it's possible to lose one's voice entirely. Soon she discovered the wonderful world of speaking with cotton softness, kids straining to hear, while teacher words register indelibly. She also found she could stand perfectly still and still effectively address every student. Her head was a gently oscillating fan. Eventually her eyes began to see everything, including every child's eyes. She learned that effective speaking was a valuable technique for classroom management and discovered how it could keep control without being controlling.

Kyrene's teacher also came to realize that the world was filled with effective speakers. Her principal was very good, especially as he spoke to a single child or to just one parent. Her fellow teachers were highly skilled communicators too. She also began to recognize that her pastor was truly a master speaker. She learned from them all. Conference speakers, workshop leaders, and video presenters were not only people who gave messages, they were professional communicators from whom she could gain insights into professional communication.

Brightened, Bound-Up, and Bridged

Speaking effectively is a powerful plus. It's a necessity for good teaching. Through spoken word the shepherd teacher motivates her learners. She brightens their lives with words of appreciation, with words that affirm and accept, and words that pick them up when they're down. She brightens with words as she strives to be positive. She understands that God is always present and always aware. God's presence brightens every situation. Knowing that He knows all one's needs helps a person cope in even the worst of times. The shepherd teacher's words bring hope and assurance to her students and to their families.

Speaking effectively is basic to good discipline. Children become bound-up in what the teacher wants. They are caught up in the desire to make things work. This happens in part because they've been led to see themselves as working parts of the classroom machinery. They've been told that they are important. Their ministry to one another and to teachers helps good things take place. Once children feel they belong and have an on-going role, they grow in self-responsibility. That's why wise teachers involve their students in a host of meaningful ways. Well-selected and well-spoken words draw them into community, bind them together, and further equip them to function effectively as a classroom of learners.

Shepherd teachers make sure that children are not inaccessible islands. Not only do teachers brighten kids' lives and involve them thoroughly, they assure them with their words that they are connected to others in many important ways. They point to relationship bridges.

Church is one such special bridge. Christian teachers stress that church draws us together. The immediate family is another bridge. Each member feels its close connection. A scout group is a good example of a relational bridge. A soccer team or swim club likewise.

The classroom family stands especially tall on the bridge list. Teachers work to help each child fit in and feel good, to make friendships and maintain them, to experience acceptance and assurance. A child feels bridged to a room, its occupants, and particularly to the important person who runs it.

The shepherd teacher skillfully speaks in order to motivate, to discipline, and to get things done. Children are inspired, they're wrapped up in what the teacher wants for them, and they're involved with those around them as they go about their work. They're repeatedly brightened, relationally bonded each day, and constantly brought together. Words are the work horses. Their skillful use brightens, binds, and bridges.

Speaking with Respect

The shepherd teacher chooses to use a language of respect and to deliver it in a respectful way. His whole body is involved. He knows that there's a one-on one counseling time when it may be perfect to slouch and slur, but that's not his classroom style. He realizes how easy it is to tease kids, but he deliberately avoids it. The door to disrespect swings wide when you tease. A respectful voice is not only the best way to get through to a child, it's the surest and best way to keep that child happy and growing.

It takes technique. It takes practice, and it takes the recognition that certain negative words and phrases, gestures and looks, are simply counter-productive and hurtful.

Speaking with respect requires proper thinking. I like to explain that all important thinking through what I call the ambassador theory.

It works like this. My principal tells me I'm getting a new student. She's excited. She quickly adds that the father of my new child is the Ambassador of Sweden. That quickly plugs in a wave of thoughts. This new kid sounds pretty special. He's part of a distinguished family. This child's dad is the personal representative of the sovereign head of an entire country. Here is a kid that's pretty important. His dad is the Ambassador Extraordinary and Plenipotentiary of Sweden. That's impressive. I've gotta' watch what I say. There's no way that I'm going to blurt out, "Hi, chubby," just because my very first thought is that this kid is too fat. Instead, I'll be super considerate. I'll speak with care. I'll do so because my thoughts are grounded in care.

Of course, not many students have a parent who is representing a foreign nation. Each child, however, is truly special and is indeed a bridge person to a house, an oft-foreign family castle.

Little Lomeka Lewis, whose mother lives near Long and Le Moyne, is worthy of major respect. She's a member of the Lewis family. One day Lomeka's teacher will use her bridge of respectful thought and word to speak the right and bright evangel words of the Gospel that the Holy Spirit will use to bring the Lewis family to the Lord.

Speaking with Love

During my internship year of teaching I learned that my classroom words could switch dramatic gears. I had become angry with the fourth grade half of my morning Grades 4 and 5 class. I was chewing them out royally for some misdemeanor when my eyes fell on John's soft doe eyes. His puzzled and hurt expression brought me up short. "Why are you turning on us like this, teacher?" John's countenance asked.

And my response was quick. My voice did a one-eighty. It had to. My heart caught up with my temper and throttled it, and provided me with words of love. I apologized. My fourth grade troops were quiet. To a heart they heard my repentant plea. They delivered non-verbal absolution, quickly, quietly, and quite totally.

Over the years I've heard hundreds of teachers speak words of love in dozens of ways, and those phrases and sentences hugged their children's hearts with affection and care. It's marvelous to hear. To the chance passer-by it may seem a bit of a bid for an Oscar, but to the principal with one ear open it's just plain love, it's a skilled teacher speaking acceptance.

Love words take plenty of practice, perhaps because they are so special. Take, for example, the typical spouse. Although married for years, he may still blanch when his mind tells his mouth to say "I love you," to his wife. Although thirty years old and plenty mature, the adult child has trouble saying "I love you" to his parents. It takes doing it. It takes practice.

Shepherd teachers are daily on stage. They have a flock audience that awaits their words. Their sheep need a safe and secure place to graze. Words of compassion create that setting. Even when being defied by a classroom denizen, the teacher can communicate compassion and care. It's a special kind of work.It takes practice.

Shepherd teachers are a lot like the parents they daily replace. The wise mom and aware dad speak love sentences lots. We listen to any good and caring parents and we hear it. Their address to a child is like a warm smile. We learn as teachers to emulate their affectionate regard. We learn to practice what we have often preached in their direction. Like them we fashion the forum and the words to deliberately communicate our care. It's intentional. It's habit forming.

Speaking to Win and to Keep

Almost every day the classroom teacher does some preaching. These are special times when a Christian teacher deliberately employs a stronger voice, one more akin to the convincing and forceful words we relate to the Sunday pulpit. There's a bit of an evangelist in the vocal wings. It's not in the volume. It's not scary. It's not even strange. Rather it is a voice proclaiming God's Word with sincerity, certain of the promises God expresses in His Word. The student parishioners are captivated by a special message moment. They are led to feel absolutely certain that God loves them and that He wants them to witness and work for Him.

Awe has been engendered. Young hearts have been touched. God is important. Our sinfulness is real and a very real wall between the Lord and those He wishes to hug. But Christ has crashed through. The cross has leveled the wall. God sent Jesus. He gave His only Son. He did so out of a love we can't measure or comprehend. Thank You, God. Thank You, Jesus. Help me, Spirit, to spread the word.

In my second year of teaching I was invited by Ben, my Bible class mentor and good friend, to attend a Billy Graham rally service at Chicago's McCormick Place. Although he was two football fields away, the Rev. Graham was a compelling magnet. What an evangelist! What a spiritual influence he's been over the years in bringing listeners to spiritual realization and in helping them make spiritual decisions. Shepherd teachers need that kind of voice at times. When presenting a scriptural classroom message that calls for witness and proclamation we find, and use, our compelling and forceful shepherding voice.

112

I love to listen to Paul Harvey. Who can do the news better? What an evangelist he really is! When he does his True Value Hardware commercial I'm ready to reroute my morning commute and drive right over to True Value. A teacher learns to be a spiritual Paul Harvey, to pace and power her talk, to package words for Christ. Consider the worth. Count and capture the true value of witnessing to kids that Jesus is Lord. Imagine further the double worth of being an instrument in bringing a child's parent to faith. What a spiritual value for that child whose parent becomes a believer in Jesus too. At just the right times the teacher shepherd speaks to win and to keep.

Speaking in Truth and for Truth

As I give a children's message during a worship service or at a school chapel, I get more response from children on one theme than on any other. Stated positively, it's when I'm talking about truth. Noted on the sin side, it's mention of dishonesty. Kids lie a lot. Whenever the Law-focus of my message is on lying, children suddenly listen more closely.

The classroom shepherd employs three truth serums. First, there's one that ministers to the children. They need to receive forgiveness. They need help in becoming more truthful. Secondly, teachers must constantly discipline themselves to be always speaking the truth. They are models. Untruth is never acceptable. Finally, it is of great value to recognize that truth plays an important role in the emotional health of both children and adults. Seeing and accepting the truth about a personal problem or shortcoming is a big help. Excuses are not.

Shepherd Jesus promoted the truth. He talked about it often. He clarified things that were fuzzy. He spoke against untruth. Furthermore, He described Himself as the true light. He said He was really God. In John 6:32 Christ followed His "I tell you the truth . . . "

with the word that His Father had given the true bread from heaven. Christians believe it. We also hold that a genuine and true spiritual life has been given us through Christ. Jesus speaks of Himself as the true vine in John 15:1. That He is. Through Him we truly do connect with God, and we truly do bear good fruit.

113

There's a lot of skill involved in speaking to the flock with respect and love, with witness and truth. Our shepherding is a serious business. We must do it well. We want to brighten, bind up, and bridge our children in the true faith and in the true church, to ground well their relationship with their Good Shepherd. It will take concentration and care.

Notes

1. John Powell, S. J., *Will the Real Me Please Stand Up?* (Allen: Argus Communications, 1985). Powell along with psychotherapist Loretta Brady sets out 25 basic attitudes and practices for effective human communications. This 234-page paperback is an excellent guide for shepherding teachers as they strive to listen and speak in love and wisdom.
2. Ken Davis, *How to Speak to Youth and Keep Them Awake at the Same Time* (Loveland: Group Books, 1986). Davis covers in detail what he calls the three truths about good communication. 1. Excellent communication skills only come as a result of very hard work. 2. Good communication can be learned. 3. There is a missing element in most speech communication courses—the *heart* of good communication.

CHAPTER 11

Seeking the Flock

Beheld and Bidden, Baptized and Belonging

The church is all about people. That's why Jesus came into the world to save people. The shepherd teacher has a heart for people. Each person is beheld as a creation of God, one the Lord claims as His child.

Shepherds concentrate on sheep. The flock is their business. They delight in caring for its needs. The birth of a new lamb is a joy. So is the addition of a sheep full-grown. Each is a treasure. None should ever be lost.

Shepherd teachers make people their first priority. People are beheld as what matters. Schools are for children. Each child is of inestimable value. Families count. They are more important than facilities or policies or positions. None should be lost to the Lord. Even the littlest person is to be seen as a very important person. That's the way Jesus saw things as He did His shepherd teaching. That's the context in which Matthew has Jesus teaching the pointed and poignant story we've tabbed as "The Parable of the Lost Sheep."

Matthew 18 Is about People

Shepherding people follow certain maxims and Matthew 18 declares strongly that the church has one principle fully in place. Every effort is to be made to care for the weak. It's an incredible chapter, one Christians respect and revere and teach a lot. The chapter ends with Christ's parable about the unforgiving servant, that unbelievably self-centered satrap who nails his fellow servant for one 600,000th part of that which he has just been forgiven. It's an outlandish example of despising a "little one" (v. 6), and clearly he has no concern for a sheep that may have "wandered off" (v. 12). He is himself forgiven up to "seventy-seven times" (v. 22), but he fails to forgive even once.

The chapter begins with an intriguing question. It helps us see people as Christ would have us see people. "At that time the disciples came to Jesus and asked, 'Who is the greatest in the kingdom of heaven?' "

Who would God say is the most important person in the world? It's a good question, one that one of your own students might well ask. It's one you could well ask your students. It gets us thinking about presidents and prestige, and about money, the military, and great learning. But who dares even contemplate, let alone follow, the dictum of Jesus that childlikeness is the only greatness.

That's Christ's surprising response. First, He calls over a child and has this little person stand there. Next comes His unexpected answer, one which undoubtedly stunned His disciples. "I tell you the truth, unless you change and become like little children, you will never enter the kingdom of heaven." Be like this trusting little kid was the gist of His reply. "Whoever humbles himself like this little child is the greatest in the kingdom of heaven," was what He stated further to drive His point home.

And there was more. "Whoever welcomes a little child like this in My name welcomes Me." Jesus was on a roll. For all time, He made it clear that to minister to a child, or indeed to any "little one," is to serve Christ Himself. Kids count. People are important. Jesus really meant it. The threat that followed made His emphasis very clear. "If anyone causes one of these little ones who believe in Me to sin, it would be better to have a large millstone hung around his neck and to be drowned in the depths of the sea."

Children are not to be hurt. They're not to be misled. They're not to be caused to stumble. The sin of causing them to sin is viewed as a major matter. Christ doesn't even want the body to come to the surface for the burial. A "large millstone," one ordinarily drawn by a horse or donkey, would take care of that.

Several sentences later Jesus added still more to His emphatic rejoinder. "See that you do not look down on one of these little ones. For I tell you that their angels in heaven always see the face of My Father in heaven." Every child, every seemingly drab or un-important person, has an angel, a powerful helper who has constant access to God Himself. That's status.

And then Jesus moved right on to tell the parable of the lost sheep. Matthew's report of it is as follows: What do you think? If a man owns a hundred sheep and one of them wanders away, will he not leave the 99 on the hills and go to look for the one that wandered off? And if he finds it, I tell you the truth, he is happier about that one sheep than about the 99 that did not wander off. In the same way your Father in heaven is not willing that any of these little ones should be lost (Matt. 18:12–18).

Behold and Bidden, Baptized and Belonging

Jesus' parable makes it plain. The Father does not want a single one of His littlest or lowliest disciples to be lost. Our heavenly Father has only one mindset. He wants to save. Each sinful person is dear to the Shepherd's love.

A person who leaves the flock leaves the Shepherd. Yet that person is still precious in Christ's eyes. No journey, trouble, or pain is too great if it helps to bring that person back to the Lord. That's what the Gospel tells us of God. God has only one desire regarding those who are lost—to save each by His grace.

Shepherding for the Lord is a matter of mission. A shepherd teacher is being a missionary, one whose main work is to nurture. Outreach and nurture both must get done. In the Great Commission the Lord did not say, "Make disciples and then forget them." He also didn't say, "Teach them to obey everything I have commanded you, but forget about anyone who hasn't come to your classroom." As co-missioners of the Gospel, partners with Him, we take seriously that we are to "Go and make disciples of all nations, baptizing them in the name of the Father and of the Son and of the Holy Spirit, and teaching them to obey everything I have commanded you" (Matt. 28:19–20).

And the promise is attached. "Surely I am with you always, to the very end of the age" (Matt. 28:20). God is with us in our work. He empowers us in and through His Word.

Shepherd Seekers Are Equipped

The basic ingredient for seeking the lost is the use of God's Word. Baptism, linked as it is with God's powerful Word, is part of the same terrific package. Equipped with Word and Sacrament, shepherd teachers have what it takes to be missionaries. The same Word that God the Holy Spirit uses to kindle and nurture faith in the hearts of the unbelieving is what strengthens and equips the shepherd who teaches and uses that Word.

The way the apostle Paul described this mission for the church at Corinth was to call the people his letters of recommendation. "You yourselves are our (Paul and Timothy) letter, written on our hearts, known and read by everybody. You show that you are a letter from Christ, the result of our ministry, written not with ink but with the spirit of the living God, not on tablets of stone but on tablets of human hearts" (2 Cor. 3:2–3). God is with His shepherd teachers as they speak and teach, witness and care. He will bless them through His Word to be able to communicate His Word. They'll be His messenger people. It will work.

So Shepherds Seek

A shepherd seeks. It's one more thing a shepherd does that makes a shepherd a shepherd. It comes with tending sheep. Sheep wander away. They're famous for straying, for roaming beyond the shepherd's view. So shepherds seek. They search relentlessly in every direction.

Listen to the shepherd as he hurriedly heads to yet another rock. How could I have been so stupid? Hear him mutter as he condemns his carelessness. If I had only thought about it earlier. Had I just not taken the flock for granted. If I had counted the sheep earlier, as I was supposed to, I would have been all right.

Anger follows frustration. He curses his thankless and demanding job. He curses the sheep. He curses the day he was born. His breathless words bespeak his panic. His thoughts scurry. I've done it now! What will the owner say? How can I face him? What will he do? It will be a great economic loss.

"I'll lose my wage," he moans. And likely my job, his harried mind responds.

I recall that very kind of anxiety on a spring Sunday afternoon in Chicago. Twenty-five years have gone by, but the panic returns in a moment.

"She wasn't with Kim and Laura and I can't find her anywhere," my wife Priscilla cried, and a neighborhood hunt was on for daughter number 2, two-and-a-half-year-old Kari. Priscilla's despair soon became mine as well. Together our distraught hearts prayed. Only 90 minutes went by, but the sense of hopelessness was complete.

What immense joy and relief when we found Kari. She'd been trapped in the rarely-used front entrance of our three-flat apartment building. The front door was locked and the previously-ajar door behind her had clicked shut. Frightened and bewildered, Kari was found, and she was okay. How that lamb was hugged and held and prized!

And why not? Losses are tough to handle, whatever they are and whenever they come. Losses in terms of people are tougher by far, especially if the individuals involved are ones that are close to us and loved. Love heightens loss. So does responsibility. Responsibility coupled with love reaches deep into our hearts.

Out of the shepherd teacher's heart comes compassion that is upset by loss and that gives impetus and energy to seeking. Teachers of the church are busy with the task of nurturing, but they must also recognize outreach roles and responsibilities. Feeding the flock is no small part of the work, but just like "leaving the ninety-nine," the nurture work must be set aside at times in order to seek the one that is lost.

There Are Lots of Ways to Get Lost

Likely every teacher has had at least one field trip experience during which someone ends up missing—a child, a group of them, or a parent chaperon. Someone got left behind at the elevator, or took a wrong turn, and is temporarily out of sight. We work hard on our trips to the museum to avoid that very thing. But not all the stories about lost children have to do with being physically missing. Let me share some others.

Little Larry is lost in the maze of his classroom's demands. He loved preschool. Larry enjoyed it all. Kindergarten seemed to go pretty well too. First grade, however, has become quite another thing. There is so much to do every day. Larry never seems to get things done. He's usually not finished with one thing and Mrs. Mandible is already moving on to the next. Try as they might, Larry's parents can't seem to help enough at home either. Here we are in

119

February and Larry is seriously behind. Larry's lost. He hates going to school.

Mary is behind, too, but she's lost in another way. Her family just moved here, and between her shyness and the reality of the fourth grade girls' established relationships, she's been unable to make any friends at all. Mary is miserable. She misses the boys and girls back in Missouri. *Mary's lost in a social sense, and it's no fun.*

Brett is dealing with an even harder loss. His mom was shot and killed during a holdup in his dad's store. Meanwhile, his dad was badly injured in the shooting and lies unconscious in the hospital. Brett and his little brother Brian are staying at a friend's house in a nearby suburb. *Brett has lost the security of family and it's hard to tell what emotional toll this tragedy will take.*

Earl is in grade 8, but you'd never know it by looking at him. Even when he slides his whole body down his classroom chair, his feet have trouble touching the floor. Earl's stretching it when he claims to be four foot seven. He's the shortest kid in eighth grade, and he's keenly aware of it. *Earl's lack of height is both an emotional and relational concern.* How he prays that he'll soon start to grow! (It really hurts to be so much littler than Cassandrah. She'll surely say no if he asks her to dance with him at the party next Friday.) Earl feels there's no one else in the whole world who has his problem.

Dee Dee's defiance is due to her parents' fighting. There's no easy way for a seventh grader to tell anyone that her dad hits her mom. There's no way for Dee Dee to know that anyone else has to deal with anything so awful. Who could guess that the big bruise above her right elbow was caused by a hard smack? She had tried to protect her mother. She seethes as she thinks of it. If she had a gun, she'd kill her father. *Dee Dee is lost in the despair of her tragic home life.*

Larry, Mary, Brett, Earl, and Dee Dee are lost in ways common to children. The alert and caring shepherd teacher is as likely as anyone to spot the problems. Larry has become obstreperous and unmanageable. Mary looks so sad. Brett daydreams a lot, and Earl was caught dealing crack over at Roosevelt Park. Dee Dee is sullen and angry. Problems are antennae for the aware teacher. When something seems seriously amiss with a child, the teacher instigates the special seeking needed to "find" the child.

And Then There's Really Being Lost

Tawfic and Faiz just enrolled at the urban Christian day school a half block from their apartment. The Musseds came from Yemen just three years ago. They're doing well with their convenience store business and are pleased to have the twins accepted into a private school.

"The children of that school behave well," Al-Maweri told his wife. "I see them in their blue pants and the girls all wearing the same checkered dresses and I like that. Good kids." Their happy smiles and their uniforms have communicated a security to Mr. Mussed. It really doesn't matter to him that this is a Christian school. His parents are Zaydi Shiites and very faithful to their Moslem beliefs, but he and Maydi have decided that they and their children will not be chained to the traditions of their homeland.

Tawfic and Faiz are lost. They don't know Jesus. This Christ the shepherd teacher knows so intimately is totally unknown to them. They have yet to hear of the God of Adam and Moses and Miriam, Abraham and Sarah, David, Deborah, Isaiah and Amos, and of Mary. These two little kids are a half block away from salvation, but at this moment the place called heaven is out. Spiritually they are dead. Should tomorrow's lot be a physical death, we know the awful eternal verdict. It's hell.

Christians hate to talk about hell, to even mention the word. It's too awful to contemplate the pain of it, the cold pallor of total separation from God. While the world may snicker at the absolutes that we Christians continue to purport, our Lord's word is clear. The deep recesses of our faith and conscience and knowledge speak back to us clearly. Where there is no relationship with God, there is no hope, no heaven. That's really lost.

The classroom shepherd must realize and authenticate the horrible prospect of eternal death and damnation in hell. As much as we might envy the comfort level of those who dismiss hell as myth, God's truth remains. We mustn't allow ourselves to be lulled into a forgetfulness of what is true. *Minus faith in Christ we're dead. There is then no saving relationship with the Father, our Creator.* That's it. What a compelling and powerful reason for our witness and word. We want Tawfic and Faiz to be in heaven. We know that .it can happen in the Gospel. We have to seek the ways to bring them the Good News that the Good Shepherd wants them found, and wants them to be in His flock now and forever.

The Church Has What It Takes

God's family of believers, the church, is centered on the Gospel. Like the hub of a wagon wheel, this Good News holds everything together. Every spoke of life makes sense when it is connected to the message of God's love and forgiveness. This is what happens as Christians gather to worship and study, to fellowship and serve, to witness and play, to celebrate and live together in trust and hope. That's why the shepherd teacher draws the lost to church. Here in the congregation and its various groups the Gospel becomes as real as life. Church is the coming together of people who celebrate God's presence in their lives, and want to help others to do so as well.

Our church schools help that happen. Through the Christian teacher and principal and staff, the church school family is brought into touch with the church, a family of families. Often today, students come from families far different from the "typical" Christian school family of years ago.

Jane Fryar stresses the change that has occurred in the makeup of Christian school enrollments when she writes about the families these schools touch in her excellent book for teachers in Christian schools, *Go and Make Disciples,* (St. Louis: Concordia Publishing House, 1992). She shares a story about Christie, who left the teaching ministry less than 10 months after the first day in her new school. Christie's plight included school family problems and behaviors she had not expected. More than half her students came from non-churched families. Sixty percent lived with a single parent. "Several parents punctuated every conversation with profanity; three or four parents had even sworn at her on occasion" (p. 174).

Fryar follows her story about Christie with the following observations:

> *Perhaps those who serve in Christian schools do not stop often enough to analyze their role, but it has changed dramatically during the past decade, and it continues to change. In the past some Christian schools may have served as enclaves, as sanctuaries that protected church member*

*students (and teachers, too, for that matter) from the fury
of sin outside. Today, though, Christian schools have become
mission fields, and those who teach there have become front-
line missionaries—front-line missionaries in the full sense
of the term.*
*Each family that comes to us brings a bundle of needs. No
school and church staff can meet all these needs. But above
all, we pray that the Lord Jesus would use us as His tools so
that by His grace He may meet their deepest need—the need
to know Him as their Savior, to know Him in a personal
life-changing way" (p. 175).*

Families need churches. Churches need families. Shepherd
teachers help each of their families become involved in a congregation so they become an active part of a larger spiritual family.
Teachers need to be familiar with three particular kinds of school
families. It will help them bring the people witness to each family.

Three Distinct Church-Membership Messages for School Families

*The first type of school family is actively involved in a congregation
of believers not connected with the school.* They attend its worship
services on a regular basis. They're being nurtured. They're growing
spiritually. It seems to be a good fit. The shepherd teacher communicates her happiness about this involvement. It comes out like
this: "Mr. and Mrs. Petrenka, we're delighted that you have strong
ties with the folks at Faith Baptist. Bless you. You and your children
are growing closer to the Lord through your membership in that
congregation. Great. We're delighted at this congregation's school
to do all we can to help that relationship grow even stronger. We
have no desire or intent to draw you away."

Where things are going spiritually well for a school family, a
Christian school need only serve as a place of support and encouragement regarding church membership.

*The second type of family has a church membership that is not
working well.* The child's application blank lists a church, but the
family is rarely in attendance. They don't feel they belong. The
relationship has gone stale. Perhaps it wasn't well-established in the

first place. A different message is appropriate for this family. "Since things are not going well for you over at St. Mel's, we'd be delighted if you'd visit with us. You already know a lot about our church because you're a part of our school. Please feel free to attend our worship services and any of our fellowship activities. Check us out. We may be just the right solution for your family's spiritual needs. Our Sunday school and vacation Bible school, I know, would work very well for your children. They have plenty of friends there already. We use the same kinds of Christ-centered curriculum materials in those programs as we do in our day school."

A lukewarm church relationship may be as much a detriment to a family member's faith life as a help. For some families, joining a new congregation is a healthy option. That's particularly true if the new church has a thorough and well-taught information course based on the Bible for all its new members, and if it has a deliberate and effective assimilation program.

The third example is the family that has no church membership. This family needs to hear a special message, one of compassion and acceptance. What they need to hear goes well beyond an ordinary invitation. They need to be bidden in a fuller way, one that vaults over the preliminaries of becoming a church member and bestows a relationship. It sounds like this: Since you don't have a church, we are your church. Although you've not taken steps to become an official part of our congregation, please think of us as your church family. By having children in our school you are very much a part of us. We appreciate your involvement and support. You're welcome to worship with us, serve the community along with us, and come to our various activities. Should you need some special ministry that we ordinarily provide, do think of us as your church. If, for example, you or your child becomes hospitalized, please let us know. We'll visit. We'll pray. We'll help out. And, most assuredly, as you might like to learn more about Christ, or about what our church teaches, we'd love to help. Consider us yours, your church home. We'd be pleased.

That kind of thinking has heart, and it will be blessed. That family is being hugged, and with the power of Christ's Gospel and the Spirit's direction, the family members will be drawn into the church.

On a recent visit to a west coast school, I heard a moving story about a young Chinese-American family. While not church members at West Portal, the family did have two children in the congregation's day school, one in grade 7 and one in grade 4. They also had a three-year-old, but this child would never get to attend the school. Tragically, their youngest child had died the previous week.

West Portal swung into action. They behaved as if the Chins were fullfledged church members. The pastor and staff ministered to them in the midst of this sad circumstance. This school family had no church membership, but they did have a church home. They had spiritual care. This family was not shuttled elsewhere because it had not yet gone through a course or a rite. It had an immediate need, one with great spiritual ramifications. It also had a church home, one it will likely join in the months or years ahead.

Teachers of church schools, along with their administrators and the church's membership, learn to focus on a school's nonmember families in one of the above three ways. Each of the three messages has its place. Each affirms the value of a church membership. Congregations, after all, are for hugging families, for nurturing them in the faith, and for helping them to be strong and effective. Congregations bid families to join their ranks in order to help them grow in the Lord. Inviting those who have no church to become a part of the church is something congregations do. It's called evangelism. It's leading people to Jesus, so that believing in Him, they can have a full life here and eternal life in heaven.

Schools of churches are not just schools. They are as much the church as the churches that sponsor them. Just as a congregation is in mission as it strives to carry out Christ's Matthew 28 command, so is the church school. Just as any Christian pastor is truly a missionary of the Gospel, so also is the church school teacher such a missionary. Pastors and teachers and other church staff usually have a ton of responsibilities, but none may be more crucial than to recognize themselves as mission workers, and to then carry out their evangelism tasks with skill and care.

Effective Seeking Calls for Intentionality

Effective people prioritize as they go about their tasks. Choices must be made. That's also true in the work of outreach. The shepherd left the 99 to seek the one. Finding the one lost sheep became the shepherd's top priority. An element of focus enters into a shepherd's understanding of evangelism. It's called *intentionality*.

I know a Christian teacher who has become very intentional regarding Baptism and the children in her second-grade class. She has also become the baptismal sponsor for quite a number of those children. That's not accidental and it's not just a matter of honoring a teacher. Those parents have invited her to participate in their child's Baptism because she's the one who first discussed with them the meaning of Baptism and introduced it as a possibility for their child.

Consider the various ways that intentionality becomes a part of getting an unbaptized child baptized. A teacher must first find out if students have been baptized. It's usually a part of the child's application and cumulative forms. Those who have not yet been baptized now move into focus.

Prayer enters the scene. The teacher asks the Lord to be with these children and to bless them as they hear His Word and grow in faith. May her questions and conversations be blessed, too, as she intentionally discusses Baptism during home visits and parent conferences. May the Lord lead her to talk with others who can pray for the children or talk to their parent(s). The principal may be just the person to make a house call on the family. A pastor may be just the one to whom the parent(s) need to be directed. The process is different for each child. It takes focus and dedicated effort. It takes shepherding.

At times a school parent, too, is unbaptized and needs to be encouraged and nurtured in special ways. Two wonderful things occur during this process. One, the baptized child gains a spiritually stronger family in which to be raised. Two, another person has become a child of God. The teaching shepherd praises the Lord for being able to have a hand in each. It's a skilled hand, one with an appreciation for intentionality in the process of seeking the lost.

Understanding Those Who Are Apt to Stray

Shepherds do need to know their sheep. Those with a penchant for straying will get close attention. Early intervention can prevent straying. The shepherd's watchful and well-timed redirection will help keep that erring one with the flock.

Shepherd teachers need to know people. They can't be naive.

Peter's appeal to the church elders of young Christian congregations applies. "Be shepherds of God's flock that is under your care, serving as overseers—not because you must, but because you are willing as God wants you to be." Teachers in ministry with the whole church staff share in the responsibility of the congregational flock with a special focus on the families that are a part of their current classroom scene. They need to understand people and how they can go spiritually astray. Alert shepherding can ward off dangerous habits. Well-timed nudges can help keep people on stronger spiritual pathways, close to the congregational flock.

People Flirt before They Stray

People who begin slipping away from church, and from the Lord, often do so because other relationships and concerns have begun to replace those that the congregation has provided. These new "others" have usually become a gradual part of their lives. It's important to effective shepherding to recognize the flirting that may be going on in people's lives. Early contact regarding spiritual implications is in order.

Cal is an excellent volleyball player. He's been invited to join a team that plays in weekend tournaments both in town and in nearby cities. The tourneys will take him away from Cindy and the children, and he'll miss church, but he'd really like to play. The diversion, he believes, will be good. It'll take his mind off work and he'll get back into top physical condition the way he was in college. Cal is flirting.

Pamela has to decide about the new job offer. Her part-time position at Quality Fabrics has worked well. The opportunity to become assistant manager is a delightful surprise. But she'll have to work evenings every Tuesday and Thursday, and that's troubling her. It would mean giving up choir and the weekly care-and-share group she and Art joined in February. Both have been really helpful to her spiritually, but she could give them up she supposes. It would give her less time to help the kids with their homework, but Art never helps them at all. Maybe he'd become a better father if she wasn't there. Pamela is flirting too.

Ramon and Carmen are getting the little house next door ready for renters. It's absorbing a lot of their time, especially weekends, but things are coming along. They've missed church every Sunday the last several months, but no big deal. Ramon doesn't seem to care that he's missed his ushering Sundays. The kids don't mind missing Sunday school, and they do worship on Wednesdays at the day school, Carmen muses. She doesn't like to miss communion, but she needs to help Ray. He hates to work alone. Ramon and Carmen are flirting with spiritual delinquency. It'll hurt.

Sarah finds being a single parent a demanding task. She's been divorced for three years. Bob helps with finances. He covers the kids' school tuition over at church and buys their clothes. It helps. Sarah has been dating Max on a steady basis. He seems to really care for her. He's sensitive, gets along great with the children, and is certainly generous. He's invited her to spend the weekend at his lake cottage. Sarah is uncertain. Max is really nice even though he's not a Christian. Sarah is flirting. (And with a lot more than Max.)

Janet and Scott get frustrated every time they talk about church. It's amazing how quickly Janet has grown away from her new congregation. Janet's disappointment in chairing an unsuccessful building-fund drive has been hard to overcome. Half her team captains let her down. No one at church has said a thing to her about the disappointing results. They probably think she's a real jerk after all she said about reaching goals and motivating people. Scott thinks she should just go to a new church. The kids aren't doing that well in school either. Maybe they ought to put them back in the public school. Janet is flirting with a poor witness for Scott. (This is not what her nonmember husband needs.)

It's crucial that a shepherd with relational and spiritual strengths be able to detect problems at an early stage. Was the straying family involved sufficiently in parish life to be missed by friends and staff at church? Will a teacher take note of poor attendance at worship services? Will someone care enough to ask? To confront? To shepherd them back into activity and proper perspective?

Teachers help. Their prayers go to work. They ask questions in order to understand what's taking place. They pass their concern on to pastoral staff. They let parents know that they are missed and encourage them to come to worship. Teachers can share how dangerous it has been for other families to flirt with people, pleasures, or perceived needs that threaten to draw them away from the Lord.

Shepherd teachers can communicate well the importance of being spiritually fed.

Unresolved Conflict Causes Relational Canyons

Conflict that is allowed to continue and grow is another cause for straying from God and the church. Some disagreement can be healthy. But disagreement and arguments can also grow into serious splits and heavy duty conflict accompanied by angry words and uncaring actions. People on both sides, perhaps church staff as well, begin to avoid each other. Lengthy avoidance takes its toll. A lack of repentance and forgiveness makes it difficult to relate to the Lord. Guilt ensues. Resentment grows. Relationships suffer. Families suffer. The church suffers.

While shepherd teachers may have had little formal training in conflict resolution, they can still minister to families in helpful ways. There's much they've learned from the Word and from conventional wisdom that applies. They can keep the following in mind:

Conflict has predictable factors.

• Those involved typically believe they know the cause, but their diagnosis is almost always in error.

• The need to be right is usually a primary contributor.

• While the people involved often feel that the conflict is rooted in action and content, it is more often caused by communication failures, particularly in listening.

• Invariably the parties overreact to words and are insensitive to feelings and nonverbal communication.

There are recognizable barriers to resolution.

• Poor judgment, anger, and the drive to be right will be present.

• Involved parties will discount an entire message when even a single flaw is found.

• Persons attempting reconciliation will encounter inattention, premature response, and a lack of awareness regarding feelings.

• It will be hard to identify issues, control damage, and retain the dignity of those involved.

Those involved will practice differing styles of conflict management.

- WIN-WIN people are collaborators. They want both parties to come out smiling.
- MINI-WIN/MINI-LOSE people are compromisers. They have something to give and something to take.
- YIELD-LOSE people are placaters. They roll over. They will accept abuse in order to keep a relationship.
- WIN-LOSE people are dominators. They are power people. With right and might on their side, they're on their way to victory regardless of cost.
- Some people withdraw. Often it's a LEAVE-LOSE proposition, but it can work out to be a LEAVE-WIN as well.

There are three stages of conflict resolution.

- At the RESISTANCE level parties will talk some and listen some. They might collaborate. They might compromise.
- At the RESENTMENT level parties complain and bitterly blame the other side. There's very little trust. Compromise has slim chances.
- At the REVENGE level the parties battle. They desire to hurt.

Positive approaches can minister to those involved and resolve the conflict.

- Conflict resolution calls for a process, one the parties agree to honor and try. The conflict manager can explain a process, such as the following one, to the parties involved.

1. Describe. The parties take turns describing each other's behavior objectively. No emotion allowed.

2. Express. Each party shares feelings honestly. Emotions will be shared, but there's no blaming allowed.

3. Stating specifics. Each party requests several specific changes. *Change is essential.* The shepherd of the process calls for repentance and forgiveness. Additional changes are good and acceptable. Be satisfied with little steps.

4. Consensus and covenant. The shepherd's goal is to bring about a cooperative and mutually beneficial agreement. The shepherd may excuse himself for part of the time. The shepherd will then work together with the parties involved to build a workable plan that will begin to renew relationships.

- Conflict resolution takes prayer. The shepherd prays. The parties in conflict pray. They promise to pray for one another.

- Conflict resolution takes patience. Count on it. It will be a lengthy process.
- Conflict resolution takes practice. Shepherds can begin with lambs in conflict and succeed easily. Sheep are much more difficult. Each time you shepherd a process, you learn something for the next.

Always, shepherd seekers realize that they are not alone in the hunt. The Lord attends our efforts. The Good Shepherd is with us. We lack for nothing. Our hands rest in His hands. The hands of others of His church offer skilled hands for helping. They'll join us in our searches as we encircle the lost and straying with God's love and wisdom. Shepherding is blessed as seeking becomes an integral part of teaching and caring tasks.

Notes

1. Jane L. Fryar, *Go and Make Disciples: The Goal of the Christian Teacher* (St. Louis: Concordia Publishing House, 1992) provides the Christian teacher a rich understanding of what it takes to disciple students for Christ with Jesus' help. As He was for the first disciples, Jesus is the example for today's teachers in Christian schools.

2. *Open Doors: Church and School as Evangelizing Community* (Minneapolis: Augsburg Publishing House, [now known as Augsburg Fortress] 1986) is a 15-minute video narrated by Mel Kieschnick that promotes the outreach of churches to school families. Every congregation is a mission congregation. Schools, pre-schools, and child care centers have enormous potential for ministry to un-churched families and inactive church members. A 24-page companion manual provides practical "how-to" ideas for improving evangelism and initiating a planning process.

3. *A Vision for Witness* is a video program available from the Board for Parish Services or Board of Evangelism of The Lutheran Church—Missouri Synod, 1333 South Kirkwood Road, St. Louis, Missouri 63122-7295. It provides a full discussion on witnessing and Gospel content. In addition, *Teacher Witness Workshops* is available from both boards to provide valuable input and skill practice in witnessing for the Christian teacher.

CHAPTER 12

Healing the Flock

Bent on Binding Up the Broken

Recall the attitude of gentleness. We found it a ready part of shepherds' hearts. Although toughened and hardened by the outdoors and by all their walking and working, we found shepherds to be tenderhearted and caring. We don't think of them as abusive and hurtful. Instead, we imagine them holding the lambs close. Their care reaches out and befriends. They have no desire to be callous and stern. Their desire is to make the best of every situation, to bless the sheep and lambs in their care.

Remember compassion too. When the needs of people become special, the sensitive shepherd's feelings match. When someone is harassed or helpless, compassion takes note. When another is desperate or depressed, compassion fashions response. When still another is in crisis, compassion calls for action. The shepherd teacher's desire to bring healing is tied to these attitudes of gentleness and compassion.

The Good Shepherd Jesus lives in our hearts. We are His good and gentle shepherd ambassadors. We carry the word of the unconditional no-limits hug and hope-filled Gospel of forgiveness and life that's in Him. We say so by faith. The help comes from God's Holy Spirit. Wayward sheep broken by sin and problems need the healing power of God. We say this by faith.

"Christians are responsible for care; God is responsible for cure." That's what Dr. Kenneth Haugk, the founder of The Stephen Ministry Series system of lay-caring, writes in his book *Christian Caregiving—A Way of Life*. Results are in God's hands. He cures. Living out the confident certainty that the cure—the healing—belongs to God is living in faith. That faith has benefits for both shepherd teachers and the lambs and sheep receiving loving care. It's neither the job of the caregiver or the care receiver to do the actual healing. Both are freed up in faith. Both can stop worrying. The one receiving care can accept help, can believe in growth, can even risk change, realizing that God will provide the cure.

But the work remains. There are still healing things to do. Ceasing to worry about who gives the healing is not a license to forget about giving care or to be careless about giving it. Developing trust takes work. Communicating acceptance takes skill and effort, and so does effectively communicating one's love.

A Lord Who Is Bent on Binding Up the Broken

"The Lord gives strength to His people; the Lord blesses His people with peace" (Ps. 29:11).

The prophet Ezekiel connected shepherding and healing with the Lord and with promises and peace. He described God's loving strength for His people by portraying the Lord as the True Shepherd. "I will rescue My flock" (34:10); "I Myself will look after My sheep" (34:12); and "I will bind up the injured and strengthen the weak" (34:16); "I will shepherd the flock with justice" (34:16); "I will save My flock" (34:22); "There will be showers of blessing" (34:26).

"I will place over them one shepherd, my servant David, and he will tend them; he will tend them and be their shepherd" (34:23). "I will make a covenant of peace with them" (34:25). "Then they will know that I, the Lord their God, am with them and that they, the house of Israel, are My people, declares the Sovereign Lord" (34:30).

God's peace was to be much more than just an absence of hostility for the ex-inhabitants of Judah. In the Good Shepherd peace becomes the fullness of life in communion with God. It connotes completeness and a harmony in every aspect of life. It's that peace that Paul describes as being beyond human comprehension (Phil. 4:7). It's that awesome. It's that special, and it's what the Lord has in mind.

Ezekiel's vision of a future shepherd made it very clear. The Lord of peace is a healing Lord. "I will search for the lost and bring back the strays. I will bind up the injured and strengthen the weak," (Ezek. 34:16) says Yahweh, the Good Shepherd. "He gathers the lambs in His arms and carries them close to His heart; He gently

133

leads those that have young," writes Isaiah of the same sovereign Lord (Is. 40:11).

God stands for healing. Jesus stood for healing. His ministry on earth gave rich evidence of love and compassion. Jairus' daughter would tell you that. So would the young man of Nain. Bartimaeus' eyes would sparkle confirmation. Raised Lazarus would shout, "Amen." The little kid with two loaves and five fish would tell you. Peter said it. John said it. So did Paul. Jesus cared for all who were broken or hurting or alienated in any way.

Healing was at the heart of Jesus' life and work. The very purpose of the manger, Mt. Calvary, and the He-has-risen! word to Mary was a matter of bringing about reconciliation and peace—healing the brokenness between people and God.

In Jesus Christ the Father's hug is a "protective custody" (Phil. 4:7 says "guards") that extends to the core of the believer's being and to the believer's deepest intention. Bringing Jesus into the lives of children and their parents and grandparents involves healing. Jesus stands for healing.

So does His church.

The Church Is a Healing Community

A suburban St. Louis congregation I once served states clearly that it stands for healing. For many years now every week's worship bulletin has earned this paragraph about its ministry:

> We see our ministry in terms of touching people with Jesus Christ for healing and serving as we teach the faith, reach out with the message of the Gospel, uplift one another through fellowship, care for the needs of others, and honor God through dynamic and creative worship.

Do you catch this church's vision of what it means to be in ministry? It's their plan to touch people with Jesus in order to *heal* them and *help* them. They'll do it by teaching, by reaching out with the Gospel, by relating to one another, by taking care of needs, by providing meaningful worship. They're hoping to bring healing to the people of their parish and to extend it to others through them. And well they should. Jesus stands for healing. He's in the midst of His people, and so His people stand for healing too.

Every congregation is a small version of the real world. It's made up of real people. The world's real problems show up with them. A young mom of five is distraught because her husband shot himself on Saturday. She's at worship the next day. I observed her tears and anguish, her heartwrenching sadness across the lobby. I also saw friends and relatives hold her, touch her, speak to her.They were a help. They were bringing some balm to the young woman's broken heart.

Many kinds of problems show up regularly on the parish prayer list for Sunday worship. Kenny Jordan is having heart surgery on Monday. Martha Robertson's mother had an automobile accident and is listed in serious condition at St. Anthony's. Max Pavlenks has cancer. The family of Shuichi and Yoshiko Shindo is mourning the death of Yoshiko's mother, Mrs. Rayko Sohari. Major Gil Dinello is being transferred to San Diego.

Many other problems *don't* show up as part of the worship service prayers. Gary Gaebles got fired on Thursday because he's not doing his work well due to his alcoholism. Elliot Demery was sentenced to four years in jail because he was convicted of income tax evasion. Anatol and Mary Zolkewsky decided last night to get a divorce. Rhonda McGriff had an abortion on Friday. Mary Pittmann and Cynthia Haller told their families that they are joining the local gay and lesbian organization and are moving in together. The elders had a huge argument with the pastor at Tuesday's meeting, and Chris Dingell has resigned as chairperson.

Whether apparent to all the parish or not, the congregation's members and staff are called to shepherd each of the above. Although they're experiencing an array of difficulties, all need to be led to a heightened awareness of God's presence in their lives. Each one needs the assurance that God answers prayer. All need to hear that God loves them and that His forgiveness is assured them fully through Christ's redeeming work. Each needs to hear that the church family still yearns for him or her to return to worship and to carry on helping ministries with them.

The shepherding Christian bent on healing has significant advantages. "Christian caregiving is superior to caregiving of any other kind," says Kenneth Haugk. "The primary advantage," he asserts "is depth." It's the main thesis of his afore-noted book. By virtue of Christian faith, a Christian is uniquely equipped to relate to the deep spiritual needs of others. Expertise in psychology is certainly a plus. Sociology has its place. Medicine has a lot to say. None, however, can give the complete answer. There's a spiritual component to every problem. If it's missing there's always a sizeable gap left for theology. It's up to Christians, both professional and lay, to step in and close that gap.

The Christian School as a Healing Community

The school children of the congregation's families, and children who come from other families in the area, make up a microcosm of the real world—a place filled with genuine struggles, survival needs, and very real hurts. While many kids regularly enjoy a positive day, an ample amount of success and plenty of fun, heartache and frustration, pain and brokenness, come to school too. Insecurity and fear, family dysfunction, peer rejection, and depression are realities in children's lives. Any classroom environment will contain (and sometimes produce) the stress, hassle, the unhealth, and unhappiness that area part of life.

Teachers, other staff, and school parents will truck their share of problems, pressures, and pain into the school as well. At any given time any person in any school community may have a serious need that calls for special care. That's the way it is.

But the Christian school, like the church of which it is a part, has decided advantages. It is generally a people-minded place, a caring community. It's likely to foster and display an atmosphere that acknowledges human hurts and responds to calls for special care. Awareness and concern will be there. Skills too. God is with them. His Word has called His teachers to bear burdens and to weep with those who are weeping.

An excellent monograph applies to this discussion. It's called *The School as a Caring Community.* It was commissioned by the Lutheran Education Association and written by Robert J. L. Zimmer and Phyllis N. Kersten (1986).

Zimmer and Kersten help us envision the Christian school and its distinctive advantages. They remind us that "it is a place where love and forgiveness, health and healing, are high priorities." They describe it ideally as a community "where the vulnerabilities of all participants can be exposed without embarrassment or fear of ridicule; where students, teachers, administrators, and staff come together in dynamic tension." And they add: "All who work together to make a school uniquely Christian must be aware that in *their* brokenness: 1) they, too, have a need for health and healing, and 2) they, too, have the potential to reach out to others in the spirit of Christ as 'wounded healers.'"

Zimmer and Kersten pose nine circles of concern. They suggest that each concern might be a monthly emphasis for the entire school. That's a fine idea, and it is nicely resourced by the publication's lists of "Awareness Activities: Things to Learn" and its lists of "Involvement Opportunities: Things to Do." They are pertinent and practical.

Zimmer and Kersten challenge Christian teachers to examine and improve schools as communities where health and healing is well-integrated in both purpose and program. The wise shepherd teacher hearkens to their call and says, "There are things I can do to help make it so, to help my school stand for healing."

• I can work to assure that my school really is a caring community, a place where people do care and help each other through brokenness, weakness, and pain.

• I can aggressively promote a God-pleasing life style, encouraging the good and healthy things of life and courageously taking a stand against those things that destroy life.

• I can help begin on a program to help teachers, students, parents, and staff to assume a greater responsibility for health and healing, beginning with ourselves and moving out into the community and the world.

• I can become better informed about the current issues in our society and about resources that are available to help us learn more.

• I can become involved, identifying specific people in need and posing activities and programs that are manageable on a personal, classroom, and schoolwide basis.

Healing—A Holistic Process

The shepherd teacher is holistic. That's another advantage. There's no sense to treating the spiritual separately from the physical and emotional. When a paralyzed man was lowered through the roof and into the room where Jesus was teaching, He made the man spiritually whole by forgiving his sins and physically whole by healing his paralysis (Mark 2:1–12).

God's people of the Old Testament were continually presented a holistic view of the human being. For them brokenness meant spiritual, emotional, and physical brokenness, all at the same time. Health, for the Hebrews was a divine and holistic gift. Before a person could be healed, his relationship with God had to be restored.

In Deut. 6:5 Moses teaches his people to "love the Lord your God with all your heart and with all your soul and with all your strength." Such love involves one's whole being. The Hebrew understanding of a person regarded the total being with no soul-mind-body divisions.

Jesus taught the same. Mark tells of Jesus answering the rabbi's questions regarding which of the 613 laws was the greatest. Part of Christ's response was "love the Lord your God with all your *heart* and with all your *soul* and with all your *mind* and with all your *strength.*" Jesus' teaching about our love for God suggests complete devotion. And add Luke's 2:52 description of the way Jesus matured as a boy. "Jesus grew in wisdom and stature, and in favor with God and men." He was a well-rounded person. He was healthy.

In John 7:23 Jesus refers to a holistic healing He had provided six months earlier. His miracle caused quite a stir because He healed a man on the Sabbath. Jesus referred to it as "healing the whole man," indicating that His healing was complete and that it permeated this person entirely. He used *holos* (whole) with the noun *hygies* (healing or soundness) to make that clear.

Jesus performed many other things that were holistic actions. Often they had to do with bringing a person into good health, but often He made less-than-perfect situations into better ones. The wedding at Cana needed wine. The stormy sea of Galilee needed calming. Zacchaeus needed company. Mary would need John to care for her after Jesus' crucifixion. In the post-Easter appearance of Jesus to His disciples at the Sea of Tiberias, the disciples needed to have a happy catch of 53 fish and to have breakfast when they got to shore.

No example of Jesus' holistic work can hold a candle to what was accomplished through His death and resurrection. The Greek

word *sodzo* (to save) also means "to heal" and "to make whole."
Salvation is holism. Sinfulness results in brokenness. Sin separates
a person and his Creator. Sin fractures marriages; destroys friendships, families, and partnerships; messes up ministry teams, committees, and countries. Into the brokenness comes the Good News
of Jesus Christ. It brings the hug of wholeness to anyone able to
accept it. Jesus won it at the cross. Our faith in Him and His promises
makes that win ours. Sin is gone. Our relationship with God is back.
Human relationships may still falter. Physical bodies will still suffer
pain and illness. But the ultimate healing has taken place. We go
through trials in the certainty of God's care, knowing He will work
things out for our good. Jesus stands for healing. The cross stands
for healing.

The shepherd teacher will stand for healing. She will endeavor
to be one who ministers to make brokenness whole. Her children
will hear that friends can be good medicine. They'll visit a nursing
home and talk about loneliness and friendships with the residents.
They'll learn a lot about people with handicaps and occasionally
welcome a guest speaker who is blind or a paraplegic. The teacher
will talk about poverty and hunger and homelessness, and the class
will pray and plan a canned goods offering and an offering of money
for a shelter. The teacher will seek ways to help the children understand ethnic diversity. Forgiveness will control classroom life.
Patience, truthfulness, respect, and self-control will be valued. She'll
care. The shepherd teacher will stand for healing.

The Shepherd's Presence

"God be with you," we say, and we know that He is, and we're
certain that He will be. It would be as appropriate to say, "I know
that God is right there with you at all times, so don't worry. He'll
take care of you." We realize that God is not the problem. He's not
going away or napping or resigning. The problem is that people
often forget that the Lord is always with them.

How much better for a little kid when she's completely certain
that God is right there for her as she puts her head on the pillow.
What a plus for a parent to realize that the Lord is with that same
little girl as she climbs aboard the school bus Monday morning.
How wonderful for this child to go about her day at school with

total confidence that God is with her grandfather, and will be guiding the doctors in the operating room that morning.

How valuable for us to know that Christ is with us. How much healing already occurs in our lives when we rid ourselves of uneasiness and distress. God is faithful. No question. He is.

Shepherd teachers communicate God's presence all the time. They especially do so when things go wrong. Trouble is no fun to handle alone. Furthermore, trouble never leaves you where it found you. It instills bitterness and anger, or gentleness and compassion. God is with us in every trouble, and He wants to help us become stronger as a result. We shepherds present a God who is completely on our side. With His help a tragedy becomes a triumph, a stress becomes a strength.

A Real Story about a Teacher Being There

A teacher can't be everywhere at the same time. Now where have you heard that before? It's true, of course, and any teacher can tell you many stories about times they've been there for kids and times they've not. I'll tell you about Linda and me.

The reports from the playground came quickly. Jimmy was first. He blurted his news, "Linda fell." Bill was just a little slower than Jimmy. "There's blood all over," was his step-behind contribution. Janice ran a breathless third. "Quick," she said, "help Linda."

I was out my classroom door. (Sometimes hallways are for running.) I shot for the exit nearest the playground. Guilt ran with me. I had just deposited my fourth graders outside a few minutes earlier and gone back to my room. Linda met me at the door. She was escorted by an entourage of budding EMS drivers and assistants, doctors and nurses, insurance underwriters, news reporters, and a chaplain or two.

There was blood all right. It was all over Linda's parka. It was on her slacks and hands, and one hand held Pam's yellow blood-soaked scarf to her forehead. She was smiling. Nothing rankled Linda. You had to know Linda. She was a rock. One that smiled. Moments ago she had fallen on a January Illinois playground and landed on her face. A sharpened ridge on the gravelly rough and icy surface cut like a knife.

Some quick first aid and a couple of phone calls later, and Linda and I were at the nearby office of Doctor John and Doctor Jane. Doctor John said it would be good for me to stay with Linda. "To help out," he said. He really thought that this first-year teacher should learn what happens to cuts next. Linda was smiling. I would have been happier in the waiting room with the dog-eared *Readers' Digest,* but I accepted the doctor's invitation.

I'm glad I did. I'd never seen anyone receive stitches. I had never thought of the need to deaden the area with a shot or imagined what it was like to suture a wound. I had no idea that Linda and I were being sewn together at the same time. What a bond grew between us that day as I held her hand and watched this semi-primitive, yet gentle and necessary step in the process of healing a bad cut.

It's a simple story, but it has stuck with me over the years. It taught me to be with my kids. Not every accident can be prevented by being present, but a shepherding presence does keep the lid on what a group of children is doing. It taught me that kids vary in the coping department. Linda handled her injury incredibly well. It re-minded me that a traumatic incident for one classroom child is experienced by them all. I recall the children's prayers for Linda. I also remember those sutures: A thread and a needle sewing flesh, a severe measure to insure the healing of a severe wound. I think about the closeness that developed between Linda and me. Our passing smiles during the balance of the year were very special. I'd be surprised if she'd not list me as a favorite teacher and good friend.

Run to Be Present Even If There's No Blood

Word about blood gets us moving. People respond very quickly to the physical needs of others. Seeing is believing, and the pain is plain. We run.

We must learn, however, to hustle down hallways for children during the less obvious times that call for healing. Often the problem is not easy to see. In the realm of a child's emotional life a bad cut may have its parallel in serious depression. Will we spot it? Will we do something about it and get some help, or will we let it fester until it leads to a suicide?

Relationally, a cut could be compared to a child's resentment towards a parent or a serious fight with a friend. No blood, but will we recognize the wounds anyway? Intellectually, the cut may be a failing grade or clear evidence of a learning problem. Are there no doctors to suture academic difficulties? (Of course there are.) Spiritually, the cut could be a two-month period with no church attendance, signs of a guilty conscience, or a clear and serious expression of doubt in God. Aesthetically, the cut could involve a decision to give up trumpet lessons or disappointment with every attempted art project.

The Shepherd's Healing View of Differences

Two famous Richard Hook paintings that I often see in Christian schools are "The Good Shepherd" and "Jesus and the Children." In "The Good Shepherd" gentle Jesus has shouldered a sizeable lamb. He's walking forward. His flock is close-in and following. Hook has captured nicely the strength and care that is in Christ the Good Shepherd. I love it.

"Jesus and the Children" pictures care and acceptance. The six children are clothed as Hebrew children, but each could represent a continent. Hook's children help us see a Jesus who loves kids of every size and race. There's more. The little girl that has propped her head on Jesus' right shoulder is completely comfortable. The boy behind Him on His left is intent. He's listening. He's a learner. The girl behind Him with the infant has a great smile. Jesus' full attention is on the little guy to His left. Christ's love and touch communicate warmth. Richard Hook did an excellent job.

Both paintings are helpful, but they don't put Jesus into a modern-day classroom. There's more to be said about differences than ever before. Roll in a child in a wheelchair. Bring in a child who is obese. Add one that is blind and one that is autistic. Don't stop. Bring in an obnoxious child who's been pampered by doting parents. Put in one who has an attention deficit disorder and another who is disfigured. Add a little girl who wears a prosthesis for one arm. Bring in the "normal"-looking kid with an undiagnosed learning disability. Include ethnic and economic diversity. You'd better stop before I call for 16 types of personalities and press in a bunch of gifted kids.

But don't change Jesus. He loves them all. He invites each to

142

His lap. He wants each one who is not whole to become healthy. All can be happy and have a desk in the shepherd teacher's classroom.

Timothy Was Quite a Challenge

Timothy was one of 11 children being baptized. What a joy to see him and his mom as part of the day school's February Baptism chapel service. Timothy attended the preschool's pre-K class. There was a huge difference between the boy being baptized in February and the one that had started preschool the previous September.

Timothy was a big boy. He was strong. Timothy was bright and he was mean. Within minutes on his first day he had created major concerns for the preschool director and his teacher. Timothy always preferred the toy some other child was enjoying. He'd grab it away and hit the child he'd just ripped off. In the next several days he demonstrated his ability to bite, to scream his demands, and to cry when he didn't get his way. In the midst of one tantrum he kicked his teacher. It hurt her a lot.

Timothy had become unpopular in a hurry. The children didn't like him. The director was ready to dismiss him. His mother was frustrated. This was Timothy's fourth preschool, and she'd been afraid this Christian one wouldn't work either. But she'd also seen some signs of hope. Timothy's teacher was different than others she'd encountered. Mrs. Prismann was wise and caring. She understood children, and she was every bit as determined as Timothy.

There was a reward for gross misbehavior. Timothy soon learned that it excluded him from his group's activity. He'd sit nearby. All he could do was watch. There was a consequence for each malicious misdeed. Mrs. Prismann explained that to him each time he was isolated. She was gentle and firm. She was surprisingly strong too. Whenever Timothy was out of control, she'd hold him. He'd do his best to get away, but he soon realized he couldn't. She spoke to him as she restrained him. Over and over she explained how the other children felt when he hurt them or made them angry.

Mrs. Prismann did other things too. When he played nicely and shared, she thanked him. She'd point out to him that he could make good decisions and could control himself. He liked that. She was Timothy's child-care person after the pre-K session, too, and she

143

held him in her lap and read to him. She rewarded his good behavior with puppet play. He loved her puppets. The puppets were special. They knew his name too.

And then there was Jesus. This Jesus was real nice and He also knew Timothy. He didn't like a kid's selfish actions, but He kept giving a kid another chance. He loved Timothy. He thought Timothy was a neat kid. It became special to sit in the circle and hear about Jesus. Timothy had not been one to sing, but Mrs. Prismann had a beautiful voice. It sounded special when she sang about Jesus. Sometimes Mrs. Prismann's husband stopped by. He liked Timothy. They would play catch or go outside to the playground.

It seemed a long time to Timothy, but after a while he noticed that the other children were starting to like him. He was feeling happier about his preschool all the time. When Mrs. Prismann told his mother that he'd had a good day at preschool, Timothy and Mom celebrated on the way home. Usually they'd eat at McDonald's. His mother talked to him more. She asked him questions. She explained to him why his dad so rarely came to see him. He learned what divorce means.

Timothy liked going to church together on Sundays. Sunday school was good too. Mark and Jennifer and Kyle were always there. They were from his preschool class. They were happy that he was going to get baptized soon.

William Would Need Special Help

I'd met William two other times before my race to the hospital. He'd come over to the school with Randy who was one of our custodians. William was a kindergartner at Maple Lane Elementary. Randy had talked to me about enrolling William in our Christian school in the fall. Randy had married William's mother, Trish, just two months ago. She was a waitress who worked afternoons and evenings at the Hampshire House. She had divorced William's dad three years before. Trish and William had moved into the two-story house on Bradford Street that Randy had purchased a year ago. His cleaning and painting, remodeling and repairing had made 707 Bradford a delightful home for his new family.

But everything changed in a flash. I was hurrying to Mercy Hospital's Burn Center. Randy asked me to meet him there in order to pray with him and William. Three hours earlier Trish had handed William out a second-floor window to a fireman. William was in good condition with minor burns. Trish died in the fire. I would minister to Randy and William the best that I could. The Lord would be with us.

Randy had shared in his telephone call that the police were certain that William had started the fire. He'd been playing with Randy's cigarette lighter after Randy went to work. Trish was asleep upstairs as she'd had to work late at the restaurant. What a tragedy. What a difficult thing for Randy to handle. How important it would be for little William to receive professional care. Randy too. The Lord would be with both of them. His love would make it all work out for good.

Using Healing Books for Kids Facing Big Problems

Come with me for a few minutes to the Curious Child. It's a cozy little bookshop in downtown historic Plymouth, Michigan. You'll see quickly that this is not some trendy mall-spot dedicated to big-bucks purchasers on the hunt for the latest electronic game or the largest stuffed whatever you can buy.

There's something very different about the books here. The shelf tags have categories such as epilepsy, Down Syndrome, sibling death, and mobility impairment, and there are greeting cards for kids in unhappy times.

A shepherd-teacher healer will be impressed. There's a book that was written by a child named Jason Gues. It's called *My book for kids with cansur,* and it was published just the way Jason wrote it—in pencil, misspellings and all. It makes you cry. There's *Randy Has Diabetes* by Janice Goffin. It was published in 1990 by Maverick Publications, Apache Junction, Arizona. There's Margaret Merrifield's educational story book about AIDS and HIV infection for kids age 4–8. Its title is *Come Sit by Me* (Toronto: Women's Press). Then there's a large stack of *There Is a Rainbow behind Every Dark Cloud* (Center for Attitudinal Healing Staff, Celestial Arts, 1979). You'll probably buy one. Of course, if you pick up *Little White Ladybug* by Renata Jones (Windswept House, 1990), you'll not put it down either.

Just as she does with other children's books, the Christian

teacher brings Christ and the Scripture to each one. And they join other books written by Christian authors such as Peggy Barker's *What Happened When Grandma Died?* (St. Louis: Concordia Publishing House), and Annetta E. Dellinger's *Adopted and Loved Forever* (Concordia). Dellinger has also written *Ann Elizabeth Signs with Love* (Concordia) in which Ann Elizabeth uses sign language to tell others of the God who made each person special. And there's *I Can't Talk about It,* the well-written children's book about sexual abuse by Doris Sanford, published by A Corner of the Heart, Milwaukee, Oregon.

There are books to read to children who are facing brokenness in their lives. There are books that can be recommended (or given) to parents as they prepare themselves to minister to their children. There are books to move a classroom of children to sensitivity and awareness. There are books that are good helpers, that help bring wholeness, books of inestimable value that can bring healing into the lives of children who are suffering loss, dealing with disease, or facing death.

Written Words as Healing Presence

Teachers write to their children and parents. They share joys and express concerns in clear and helpful ways. Shepherding brings the Lord into those words. Christian teachers become adept at blessing their messages. They choose and write words that minister. They convey Christ. Their constant frame of reference is the great hug of God's love and forgiveness, the Gospel. Shepherd-writing empowers. God's wonderful presence becomes clear.

A person in need of care and strength is a small boat. God is the shore. The boat can easily drift from the land, and it often does. Winds of trouble and trauma can make things worse. As the boat moves further away it is harder and harder to return. But the shore is still there.

The shepherd teacher is another little boat, but it's not adrift. It's affected by the winds, too, but it bobs up and down in place. It's anchored. It throws its little neighbor a lifeline, words of confidence and assurance. We're close to the shore. The shore will not move.

A craggy cross-anchor rests in the Christian's boat. The teacher

146

throws it out in faith and it proves incredible. The rope has no limitations. Depth and distance don't count. Prayer wings it toward the beach. It digs into the sand. The shepherd teacher's thoughts and words pull on the rope until the boat slides toward land. God the Immovable One brings the drifting one close. In Christ, the shepherd's words have helped link a child and his Father. They've come together and the teacher rejoices. She writes notes of encouragement again and again, and prays, and speaks. God brings healing.

A Letter to Heather

January 4

Dear Heather,

Hi! I was hoping to see you the day of your Great-Grandpa's funeral, but I missed you. I pray that you are doing fine.

I wanted you to know that Great-Grandpa Cecil's death made me very sad. I liked him a lot. He was a kind and gentle person who appreciated the things we do for children here at St. John's. I'll always remember him coming to vacation Bible school, your hand in his. He certainly loved you a lot so I know you will miss him and that you are very sad too.

But I know something else. I know that Great-Grandpa Hanson is in heaven now. He surely is and he is completely happy there. He has no more sickness or pain. He's in heaven because Jesus loved him enough to die for him and us again. So, even though we are sad our hearts are also happy.

Blessings to you always, Heather. Keep smiling. Enjoy the rest of grade 2. Say hi to your mom.

> *Cordially in Jesus' name,*
> *Ervin F. Henkelmann*
> *Superintendent of Childhood Ministries*

A letter of care and comfort can help the little Heathers of the world heal. They can bond people to one another. Our love does that.

Christ adds an entirely new and different dimension. His love is not at all like ours. The Gospel story is not about what people can do. If people could come into the holy presence of God by what they can do, the cross and the Scripture would be pointless. The story is about God. The Gospel story is about what God has done in His love.

Martin Marty calls it a saving story. In *Being Good and Doing Good* (p. 104) he writes, "Humans cannot sit down at word processors and idly press keys or assemble sentences and call it the Word of God. The Word of God is a mysterious but saving story about a people at the east end of the Mediterranean, about a rabbi who lived among them, about a community of believers that grew, against all reason and odds, on the soil of His rising from death to a new, immortal life."

As teaching shepherds tell the story and relate it to the lives of the lambs and sheep in their flocks, the Gospel has its effect. It builds them up. It gives them worth. Through the wondrous and lasting hug called baptism, Christ and Christians become one. God's worth has been handed over as a gift.

Teacher shepherds never tire of this saving story. It claims them and equips them. Through it, teaching ministers are called to be shepherds of God's children at that sheepfold that is theirs.

We are called to serve with an integrity of heart committed to the Lord and His people. We are to be the hands of Christ to our flocks. We do so in the full-blessed assurance that our God will make the wonderful Heb. 13:20 benediction a daily reality in Christ: May the God of peace, who through the blood of the eternal covenant brought back from the dead our Lord Jesus, that great Shepherd of the sheep, equip you with everything good for doing His will, and may He work in us what is pleasing to Him, through Jesus Christ, to whom be glory for ever and ever. Amen.

Believe it, fellow shepherds. Gather, protect, watch, lead, speak, seek, and heal your flocks in joy. The Good Shepherd is with you. Take care.

Notes

1. Kenneth C. Haugk, *Christian Caregiving—A Way of Life* (Minneapolis: Augsburg Publishing House [now known as Augsburg Fortress], 1984) provides both a practical how-to manual for Christian caregivers and the vision for what Christian caregiving is all about.

2. Robert J. L. Zimmer and Phyllis N. Kersten, *The School as a Caring Community* (River Forest, IL: Lutheran Education Association, 1986).
3. Martin E. Marty, *Being Good and Doing Good* (Philadelphia: Fortress Press [now located in Minneapolis and known as Augsburg Fortress], 1984).

About the Author

Ervin F. Henkelmann currently serves as Education Executive for the English District of The Lutheran Church—Missouri Synod. In his shepherding ministry, he has served as Superintendent of Childhood Ministries at St. John's, Orange, California; superintendent of the Lutheran Association for Elementary Education in Fort Wayne, Indiana; principal at Christ Community, Kirkwood, Missouri and Trinity, Fort Wayne, Indiana; teacher at Messiah, Chicago and Trinity, Tinley Park, Illinois; and teacher intern at Zion, Marengo, Illinois.

Henkelmann is the co-author of *How to Develop a Team Ministry and Make It Work*, (St. Louis: Concordia Publishing House, 1985) and author of numerous materials for the Lutheran Education Association. He and his wife Priscilla are the proud parents of three daughters and grandparents of two grandchildren.

About *Feed My Lambs*, Henkelmann states, "Christian learning isn't what happens for 20–30 minutes in the religion slot each day. It's the entire gathering of the school—children, families, staff—the sin/grace, Law/Gospel implications of not being conformed, but transformed by our renewal in Christ. We're committed to children as people of promise, to honor them, bless them, and build them up. Our Spirit-led commitment to the Lord breeds a desire for excellence in all we do."